UNLOCKING SECRETS

To Rich —
In truth & love
Kathy

UNLOCKING SECRETS

SECRETS

MY JOURNEY
TO AN OPEN HEART

KATHE CRAWFORD

HAY HOUSE, INC.
Carlsbad, California • New York City
London • Sydney • New Delhi

Published in the United States by: Hay House, Inc.: www.hayhouse
.com® • *Published in Australia by:* Hay House Australia Pty. Ltd.:
www.hayhouse.com.au • *Published in the United Kingdom by:* Hay
House UK, Ltd.: www.hayhouse.co.uk • *Published in India by:* Hay
House Publishers India: www.hayhouse.co.in

Cover design: Angela Moody • *Interior design:* Karim J. Garcia

Library of Congress Cataloging-in-Publication Data

Names: Crawford, Kathe, 1957- author.
Title: Unlocking secrets : my journey to an open heart / Kathe Crawford.
Description: Carlsbad, California : Hay House, [2018]
Identifiers: LCCN 2017060613 | ISBN 9781401953270 (tradepaper : alk.
paper)
Subjects: LCSH: Crawford, Kathe, 1957- | Crawford, Kathe, 1957---Mar-
riage. |
    HIV positive persons--Family relationships--United States. | Family
    secrets. | Self-acceptance.
Classification: LCC CT275.C8744 A3 2018 | DDC 155.2--dc23 LC record
available at https://lccn.loc.gov/2017060613

Tradepaper ISBN: 978-1-4019-5327-0

10 9 8 7 6 5 4 3 2 1
1st edition, May 2018

Printed in the United States of America

For my sons, Larry and Brian

CONTENTS

FOREWORD

Do you hide aspects of yourself, or pieces of your past, to present an appealing persona to the world? Do you stuff down secrets for fear of being a truth-teller? Do you feel like you're living a double life?

In my years of coaching, and years before that of my own secret-keeping, I've discovered that most of us truly believe we have to hide who we really are in order to be loved and accepted. The crazy thing is that while we all want to be loved for the truth of who we are, we greatly fear being open, honest, and vulnerable.

For most of my life, I have been seeking external validation and approval, plus outward permission to even love and accept myself. I put everyone else's wants, dreams, and needs before mine. I have spent my days managing the perceptions of others, projecting an image of perfection. In the process, I forgot something.

I forgot to live my own life.

Much of this stemmed from the secrets I was hiding and the ways I overcompensated to cover them up. Because here's the deal, we create chaos to avoid the truth and if we don't look truth right in the eye, it will come out sideways. Everything we are seeking externally must first be resolved internally.

As I've written in my books *Jump . . . And Your Life Will Appear*, *Worthy: Boost Your Self-Worth to Grow Your Net Worth*, and *The New Relationship Blueprint*, and if you're like me and Kathe, you've been abandoning yourself for far too long, living in reaction to others instead of from your own authentic, organic agency. It's now high time to take this oath: *I'm no longer willing to package myself to be digestible to others!*

As someone who has coached thousands of people to embrace fear and welcome change through truth-telling, whether it be relationship transitions, switching careers, geographical relocations, or setting boundaries, I've also made my own jumps that include a contentious divorce after a long-term marriage and quitting my prestigious position as Event Director at Hay House, Inc., to lead an entrepreneurial life as a coach, author, and speaker. I've seen that no matter what the external jump is, the internal jump is always a deepening of self-awareness, self-acceptance, self-compassion, self-forgiveness, self-love, and self-worth.

I'm glad you're here. Inside this book you'll discover the destruction that secret-keeping can do and the liberation possible when we reveal our truth. While the content of Kathe's story differs from mine and likely from yours, she weaves us into her world by sharing her devastation and her triumph—and we find ourselves within each thread.

In the present climate of whistle-blowing and #metoo, after being silenced for far too long, we know it takes more than courage to let the skeletons out of the closet. It takes a profound and intimate relationship with our own sense of self-worth.

This book is not only a love story, it's a *self-love* story.

Praise for *Unlocking Secrets*

"Kathe boldly shares her courageous journey from hiding behind a wall of secret shame to living joyfully, honestly, freely, and on purpose with a radiantly open heart. This is a beautifully clear portrayal of her sacred transformation, and we are richly blessed that she has shared it with us."

— **Ramanada John E. Welshons**, author of
Awakening from Grief and *One Soul, One Love, One Heart*

"The longer we withhold the truth, the more locked up it becomes and the more arduous is the journey of coming home to ourselves. This courageous story of the healing that is possible on the other side of secrets is a true inspiration. A well-told story with a profound message."

— **Gail Larsen**, teacher and author of *Transformational Speaking*

"This is a poignant, personal tale of spiritual awakening. Here, the ancient, folkloric tradition of storytelling becomes the healer and the healing. The secrets that Kathe shares are all of our secrets. Her generosity in sharing her own through this incredibly moving tale will provide much healing to us all."

— **Sarah Tomlinson**, yantrika and author of *Coloring Yantras* and *Yantra Bliss Oracle Deck*

"*Unlocking Secrets* is a love story on so many levels. Kathe's brave story is a giant permission slip to release the secrets that live within you, yet no longer serve you. This book will blow your heart wide open and free you to live fully and courageously from this day forward."

— **Beth Kempton**, author of *Freedom Seeker* and *Wabi Sabi*

"This is a book about what it means to courageously claim your truth and accept every single part of who you are— and to discover freedom in that process. Kathe's story is a testament to the power of unlocking our secrets and reconciling with the pain, shame, and fear in our lives."

—**Kelly McNelis**, founder of Women For One and best-selling author of *Your Messy Brilliance*

"Kathe bares her truth. She is real. She is raw. This is a great read for anyone ready to find their voice and live a more authentic life."

— **Susan Hyatt**, master certified life coach and author of *Create Your Own Luck*

"True enlightenment is to walk this path with all you have been given and turn it into a gift to share with others. Kathe is a true goddess and warrior who transformed darkness into light."

— **Sheryl Edsall**, master yoga and ayurveda teacher and founder of Naturally Yoga

"In courageously unveiling her own secrets and lies previously guarded from the world for decades, Crawford paves the way for each of us to find the true magnificence and inner peace we are all meant to be living. This is a love story for the soul."

— **Kristen Noel**, Editor-In-Chief, *Best Self Magazine*

"A raw and gripping read that shows the pain of living with secrets and that having the courage to stand in the truth can forge a path to freedom."

— **Randy Spelling**, speaker, intuitive business coach, and author of *Unlimiting You*

"Crawford teaches us that true self-love can only come with true self-expression. *Unlocking Secrets* serves as a guide for enabling us to work through the dark nights of the soul to the dawn of self-enlightenment and inner self-love."

— **Jack Schwartz**, PsyD., NCPsyA.

I've had the honor of coaching Kathe since the fall of 2015 and have witnessed her tremendous transformation firsthand. She came to me knowing she had a big, intimate story that she was afraid to tell, and before she could share it with the world, she needed to come to terms with her own shame, guilt, and fear of exposure. I guided her as she grappled with her sense of loyalty to her deceased husband and the past, and her sense of present and future self. I cheered her on, supporting her decision to leave her glitzy, glamorous, well-paying corporate profession in service of what her life has prepared her to become: a powerful and graceful teacher, author, and integrative coach.

If you've ever felt suffocated by a secret, haunted by hiding your truth, or fearful of allowing your voice to be heard, this book you are holding will illuminate your path out of darkness into the light.

My wish for you is that Kathe's story will help unlock the secrets you've been keeping and set you on the course of your very own healing journey to freedom.

Nancy Levin
Boulder, Colorado
February 2018

INTRODUCTION

*Loving yourself . . . means welcoming yourself as
the most honored guest in your own heart.*

— MARGOT ANAND

This is a love story. Not one of those schmaltzy, romantic
love stories, but a love story just the same. Do you remember that song "What I Did for Love" from the musical *A
Chorus Line*? I could just as easily give this book the same
title. Through all the drama, pain, and absurdity you'll
read about on these pages, love is the one theme at the
center of it all.

And love is also the main reason I kept secrets. I spent
a great deal of my life from childhood to adulthood as the
protector of others. I wore a figurative suit of armor in an
attempt to safeguard the secrets—as well as the demons,
pain, and suffering—of my loved ones from the world.
Doing so gave me an excuse to ignore my own demons
and suffering. I could hide from the wounded child underneath that suit of armor. I could hide my true self from the
people in my life, believing that if anyone knew the real

me, they'd run in horror, and I'd be left alone without any love at all.

It wasn't until I learned how to remove that armor from my heart that my healing truly began. Now I know there's a different way to live, and I'm ready to do the hard work of sharing my truth with the world, despite not knowing how it might change my life. After this, there will be no one left to tell. Some of what you'll read in this book is being told for the first time.

Of course, I'm in no way advocating that everyone should go out and share all of their private information with the world. Sometimes secrets are necessary. Privacy is your right. But I kept my secrets without stopping to think about whether it made sense or not, and eventually those secrets became burdens that kept me isolated and fearful.

I am someone who knows instinctively how to support and love other people. Releasing my secrets has helped me learn how to fully accept and love *myself.*

Today, I realize that it's important to decide what to disclose and what to withhold based on conscious consideration and an open heart, rather than fear. Often, we're so scared of judgment that we don't allow ourselves to be known to anyone. When we do that, we have no allies, no one to tell us we're okay, and no one to support us through the hardest times. We don't give anyone a chance to love us unconditionally. It's a terrible way to live, so a time came when I had to change.

After going through all that you'll read about in these pages, I knew my life was a mess, and all the therapy I'd been through just wasn't cutting it. So I began to meditate, practice yoga, and study with spiritual masters. I now have a spiritual practice that helps me live more fully every single day. Today, I'm an integrative life coach, motivational speaker, and registered yoga teacher. I teach workshops on discovering your truth, defining your best self, and opening your heart.

While a lot of what I've been through has been painful, there has also been a great deal of joy in my life. My experiences taught me to recognize the gift of each and every day, knowing it could be the last. Those experiences showed me how to help others using my courage, spirit, and tenacity. They motivated me to succeed and made me a master at facing life's challenges head-on.

Now, my life is completely different from that of the person you'll read about in most of this book. I'm living proof that you can change if you're determined to do so. I'm not trying to come across as a victim, a martyr, or a heroine, although I know we all play each of those roles at different times in our lives. I'm just a woman who finally woke up to her heart and continues to strive to be more awake every day.

My purpose—and my greatest hope—in sharing my story is that in it you'll find inspiration to help you question, explore, and evaluate your own life, as well as the secrets you keep.

CHAPTER 1

SPILLING MY
SECRETS

In August 2015, I was at the Omega Institute in Rhinebeck, New York, standing up in front of my fellow participants at a workshop called "Transformational Speaking." I was shaking in my shoes, getting ready to release secrets I'd held on to with a tight, unyielding grip for 30 years.

I had gradually disclosed some of those secrets to family and a few close friends. But for a long time, no one knew —not my best friend, not my parents, and not my sons.

Only my husband, Larry, knew. Because they were his secrets and I was their keeper, their guardian. In fact, I didn't really think of any of it as "secrets," per se. It was just our life. And I was simply protecting him and our family. It was all for love . . . or that's what I told myself.

But what I eventually came to understand is that I was hiding to protect myself from shame and fear of judgment. As long as I could stay hidden and not admit the truth, no one had to know who Kathe Crawford really was. By keeping the secrets, I could remain safe from the ridicule and rejection that scared me so much.

After decades, though, the thick veil of hiding became too great. So, almost in spite of myself, I was compelled to stand up and speak at the Omega workshop.

By that time, my husband had been dead for 20 years, but I was still ridden with guilt the night before I was to share our story. Would he be okay with my disclosure? Should I continue to protect him, even in death?

I hadn't had time to fully grapple with that guilt before I got to Omega because my intention had been just to listen to other people speak. I wasn't going to do it myself. At that time, I didn't care about public speaking. I just wanted to get tips on how to release the story I'd been protecting for so long. The actual release would come *later* . . . when I was really ready. *You'll just go, sit in the back, learn a few things, and go home*, I told myself.

On the drive to the workshop, I'd had an argument with myself. I'd just had a long and stressful workday and was exhausted. *Why do you have to keep fixing yourself? You've been working on yourself for years. When's it going to be enough? Can't you give yourself a break for once?* A part of me wanted to turn around and go back home—skip the workshop altogether.

Then another part of me chimed in: *Internal work is always hard, but you know you love it. You always feel better afterward. Stop beating yourself up. This will be good for you.*

Through my spiritual work, I had begun to chip away at my layers of defenses and heal a lot of my old wounds. Still, the core of my pain and the core of my true self were both safely hidden deep inside. As a result, my heart couldn't fully heal. Maybe if I could finally learn how to let go of the hiding, the healing would take place. That's why I had signed up for the workshop in the first place.

Our facilitator, Gail Larsen, spent the first three quarters of the first day's workshop talking about how to speak from a place of truth. But how's that done by a secret-keeper? *Obviously, you're here for a reason*, I thought.

Then several participants were given eight minutes each to tell their stories. By this time, I was in a cold sweat. A part of me really wanted to do it, but *I can't* was all I could think. Still, something drove me to approach Gail with a question. Trembling, through tears I asked her, "Please tell me the secret of how to do this. I'm so deathly afraid. I don't know if I can tell my story." (Ironic that I would ask for "the secret," isn't it?)

"Then, don't tell it," she said.

I was surprised by her response. "What do you mean?"

"Well, if you can't tell this story that you're telling me you *have* to tell, then tell a different one."

"No, you don't understand." I drew a line on the floor with my toes. "You see this line? It has taken me years to get here. If I don't step over that line in your workshop, I don't think I'll ever do it." I was surprised by the words that came out of my mouth. This wasn't what I'd planned at all. But suddenly, instinctively, I knew I was at a crossroads and that my life would change if I could just get over this hurdle.

"Then the only advice I can give you is to be the first one to stand up in front of the group tomorrow morning, because then your fears won't have time to build up," she said.

That night, a psychic gave a presentation and channeled some deceased people from the other side. *Maybe Larry will come through and tell me it's okay*, I thought. But no such luck. I kept looking for a sign from him. It might seem silly, but a big part of me still felt that I would be betraying him and that I needed his permission.

I stayed up past 2 A.M. trying to prepare my talk because we weren't allowed to use notes. But no matter how hard

I tried, I couldn't get my brain to focus. So I just surrendered and went to bed. *Whatever comes out is whatever's going to come out*, I told myself.

The next morning when Gail asked who wanted to go first, I raised my hand. Earlier, at the start of the workshop, everyone had worked together to create a name for each person. I had been given a medicine name, the Goddess of Love, Light, and Truth. "Truth"—it seemed to be another sign. So I started my talk by saying, "I don't know what the Goddess of Love, Light, and Truth is like, but I can tell you what the Goddess of Fear is like," and just continued from there.

I had spoken many times at work functions and always hated it. So often, I'd get lost because negative thoughts would derail my thinking. But not this time. It was the first time I had ever felt as though someone was almost talking through me. My heart opened, and it spoke. I guess it couldn't—*I couldn't*—hold it anymore. It was like that Elizabeth Appell quote: "And then the day came when the risk to remain tight, in a bud, became more painful than the risk it took to blossom."

Gail let me talk for 13 minutes instead of the usual 8, and when I was finished, I looked out at the group. There was a stillness in the room. Several people were crying. Many were smiling.

What I didn't see—but had fully expected to see—was judgment or rejection. No one threw daggers at me or left the room. Nobody was looking down on me. And while I'd started the talk afraid, I was no longer afraid. The drive to tell the truth kept me going.

I kept my secrets for 30 years based on beliefs about what might happen if I let people see the real me. But after my disclosure, my world didn't come to a shattering end.

Instead, people came up to me during our break and told me their own secrets. One woman had been raped and hadn't told anyone. Someone else had lost a job due to addiction.

A couple of them said, "You should write about this." It was the first time I'd ever considered that my story could potentially be of value to others. It seemed as though the universe was sending me a message: "This isn't just about you anymore. We all have a story to tell, and almost everyone hides pieces of who they are. Maybe you can educate people about the emotional cost of hiding and secret-keeping."

I wasn't entirely convinced, though, until a few months later in New York City. I was downtown and decided to walk over to the September 11 memorial. I had known several people who died that day in the terrorist attacks, but had never visited Ground Zero. For so many years, the thought of doing so had been just too painful. But for some reason that day, I stopped and paused at the corner, looking down at the memorial's waterfall.

Then I noticed that I'd stopped directly in front of the name James Crawford. Now, I didn't know James Crawford, but I certainly had known a *Larry* Crawford. I could feel that this was a message from my Larry. He was there with me!

I went down into the subway to head back home, and while waiting on the platform, a woman and her husband asked me for directions. We chatted a bit and ended up sitting next to each other on the train.

During our ride, my phone beeped to let me know I had an e-mail, and when I checked, I saw that it was from Hay House. I opened the e-mail to discover that my book proposal had been accepted for publication! It was impossible to contain my excitement, even though I was in public. I'm not a crier, but my eyes welled up as I was overwhelmed with joy.

It felt like a message from Larry that it was okay to share our story with the world. My heart pounded, and I just had to tell the news to someone. So I turned to the woman who had asked me for directions and asked, "May I share something with you?"

"Of course."

"I wrote a book proposal, and I just found out it's going to be published!"

"Really? Congratulations!"

"Yes! I can't believe it!"

"What's the book about?" she asked.

"It would take a while to tell you. Basically, it's about my life, but mostly about my husband's death. It was very traumatic for me. I loved him very much."

"What's your name? I want to read the book."

"I don't even know when it will come out. It'll be a long time."

"That's okay. I really want to read it."

"Kathe Crawford. Kathe with an *e* instead of a *y*. Thanks for letting me share that! And are you clear now about how to get where you're going?"

"Yes, I think so." She paused for a second and took a breath. "I'm taking my husband to the hospital for his first chemotherapy treatment. He has stage four cancer." Her eyes filled with tears, but I could tell she was trying to stay strong since her husband was sitting right next to her. He just looked at me as the three of us shared a moment of . . . I don't know exactly what to call it. Grace? Fear? Love? All of the above. They knew I understood what they were going through.

"I don't know what to do," she continued. "I just don't know how to handle all of it."

She had so many questions she wanted to ask me. I tried to answer all of them before I reached my stop.

When I had to leave the train, I hugged her good-bye, not knowing if I'd see her again, if her husband would make it, or if she'd ever read my book.

I was sure that meeting them was another sign from the universe that there was a purpose in telling my story.

"My story." It wasn't until I started sharing it that I began to fully understand what keeping my secrets had done. The release I felt that day at Omega was like taking a full breath for the first time in 30 years. The freedom I'd longed for all my life had been largely in my own hands all along. It wasn't about getting away from anybody else. It was about opening up and allowing. It was about trusting myself and trusting that there were people who would love me in spite of my past. More than anything, though, it was about learning to *love* myself. That was the biggest lesson.

And it was a particularly hard lesson because I had learned how to hide my true self and how to keep secrets for my loved ones long before I ever met my husband. I had learned all that in my childhood.

CHAPTER 2

LEARNING
TO HIDE

Growing up, I was intrigued by the front doors of the houses in our North Jersey neighborhood. My dad worked long hours, and my mom was often nowhere to be found. So I spent a lot of time wandering the nearby streets, playing a game with myself: *Whose door will I knock on today? Who will welcome me as a part of their family?*

I would sneak peeks through the windows of the houses. I imagined the kids coming home from school, their mothers greeting them with excited hugs. "How was school today? What did you learn?" You know—the kinds of things that happen in normal households. Even at a young age, I knew my family wasn't *normal*, and I wanted normal so much I could taste it.

As I tried to catch glimpses of what was going on inside my neighbors' homes, I fantasized about how the children's moms lovingly made dinner for them while they did their homework. *What would it be like to be one of those kids? If I could just get one of these families to take me in,* I thought, *I would feel safe and loved. I would matter.*

Not that I ever had the courage to actually knock on any of those doors. But the make-believe game was an innocent, comforting escape from the chaos going on behind the closed door of my own house.

From the outside looking in, I'm sure everybody thought we were an average family with a loving mother, a hardworking dad, and good kids. But that was a façade my parents were careful to present to the world. I learned early on that the truth should be hidden if you want to be accepted by others.

My parents were a good-looking couple, so it wasn't difficult for them to keep up appearances. You couldn't get more beautiful than my mother, Rosalie, nicknamed "Chickie." She was an olive-skinned second-generation Italian American who looked a lot like Ava Gardner, one of Frank Sinatra's wives and a Hollywood Golden Age screen siren. Mom had enormous dark eyes, full lips, and long, thick, fiery auburn hair.

She was the kind of woman who turned every head—male and female—when she walked into a room. Men turned to putty around her, and she loved the attention.

My dad had chiseled features with that "bad boy" James Dean kind of look. He was six foot two and slender, but also muscular, rugged, and strong. Since he was a roofer, he had a natural six-pack from carrying bundles of shingles on his back to the tops of houses.

Dad turned Mom's head as much for his earning potential as his looks. Well, that and the new baby-blue Cadillac he drove. His friends called him "Cadillac Joe."

Chickie and Cadillac Joe were popular in their community. Mom could captivate anyone with her passion and zest for life. Dad was everybody's friend—the kind of guy who would give you the shirt off his back. Despite his lack of education, he was smart, well-read, witty, and had a great sense of humor. To me, he was larger than life.

Dad had a rock-solid work ethic, but not my mom. She was the unconventional-artist type with the gift of creativity, and she didn't like to work hard.

As popular as they were, neither of them seemed to understand how to be parents. When I was older, my mother said to me matter-of-factly, "I never really wanted kids. I only had them for your father. I was a kid myself when you were born!" She was right. She couldn't handle the responsibility and just wanted to play.

Nevertheless, she had three children—my brother, Joe, who was just a little more than a year older than me, followed by me, and then my little sister, Kris, nearly a decade later. Joe and Kris got my mother's dark Italian features, while I got my father's blond hair and blue eyes.

Mom and Dad's brand of parenting often involved leaving us to fend for ourselves at a young age. For example, when I was five years old and my brother was seven, they decided we should go to parochial school and the adjoining Catholic church. "We think God is important, but we don't really believe in him ourselves or like what religion stands for," they said. "But you should make your own decisions and figure it out." How could children as young as five and seven figure out such a thing?

The school and church were nearly 30 minutes away by bus. Sometimes Dad would drive us to school early before work, but no one at home made us breakfast, so he'd give us money to buy buttered rolls at the deli next door. On Sundays, they'd drive us to church, leave us there, and pick us up after Mass.

Girls were supposed to cover their heads, but my mother had forgotten that. One of the nuns looked at me and said, "What's wrong with you? Where are your parents?"

"I don't know. They just dropped us off," I answered quietly, cringing inside as she placed a tissue on my head, shaking her head in disapproval. Even at five years old, I understood enough to feel ashamed and embarrassed.

Inside, I watched all the families there together. Their clothes were crisp and clean. The men wore suits and ties. Many of the families held hands. It was amazing. I wished I had parents like that.

Even though the nuns frightened me, I suppose my exposure to the church solidified my spirituality. God, Jesus, and the Holy Spirit were my solace and my true family. I trusted God like I didn't feel I could trust the adults around me. It comforted me to know that He was always watching over me when no one else was.

Often when I came home from school, I couldn't find my mother anywhere. I felt rejected. Why didn't she want to be with me?

Mom's local extended family was busy living their own lives, and Dad's family didn't live nearby. Plus, Mom was frequently not on speaking terms with her family members, so there were rarely other adults available to help. I couldn't get attached to anyone, though, because if I did, they'd soon disappear from our lives.

I loved my maternal grandmother, who was more of a mother to me than my mom. But she and my mother didn't get along, which sometimes got in the way of my spending time with her.

Then, when I was eight years old, I made the mistake of telling my grandmother about a fight I'd witnessed between my parents. My grandmother asked my mom about the argument, and I caught my mother's wrath for telling. It became clear that Mom wanted our family business kept from our extended family.

That's when the importance of secret-keeping was solidified for me. It certainly felt important for my own safety and became ingrained in me as a survival mechanism. I had to either keep almost everything to myself or deal with my mother's anger.

Despite this secrecy, between the five of us in my immediate family, there were few boundaries. Mom would think nothing of telling me the details of her relationship with my dad. As I got a bit older, she even casually told me she wasn't sure if she wanted to stay with him, as if I were one of her girlfriends. Little was sacred or censored. We shared pain, violence, and tears. And those shared secrets kept us tight as a family in many ways—brutally tight and emotionally enmeshed.

My mother's biggest secret was the way she behaved when only the immediate family was around. She'd have outbursts that built and built until she started smashing things—even items she loved. I don't know if Mom did it on purpose, but she often smashed gifts I'd given her. She even sold some of my gifts over the years.

"I gave you that!" I'd say when she broke things, but she'd just brush it off.

"You made me do it. Next time, behave!" The rejection was heart-wrenching. I loved her so much, and I just couldn't understand why she would treat me like that.

She blamed both my brother and me for her fits, but I seemed to be her number one scapegoat. "It's all because you didn't come home on time," she'd say, or "If you'd just vacuumed the house like you were supposed to."

I didn't realize it as a child, but she was dealing with mental illness. All I understood was that she couldn't control her rage. She also had debilitating physical illnesses starting when I was only about five. For a while, doctors thought she was just suffering from some sort of psychosomatic "female hysteria." Then she finally found someone who diagnosed her with endometriosis. She would often start to hemorrhage out of nowhere, and we'd have to rush her to the hospital. She had terrible bad luck from a medical perspective. Once, she was even dropped from a gurney and was injured.

As a result, throughout my childhood, when Mom was home, she was usually in bed and in pain, barely able to move. This was why, even after her outbursts, it was hard to stay mad at her. How do you turn away from someone who's suffering so much? What I heard in her voice was pain and desperation, and I was always so scared she was going to die. The fear of abandonment was always right on the surface.

All I could think to do was to try to help her as best I could. Since I was the girl and Dad worked late so much of the time, it became my responsibility to take care of Mom and the house.

I tried as hard as I could to do everything the way Mom wanted so we could have peace. When she stayed calm, caring for her fulfilled me in a strange way. I'd brush her brow and ask if she was okay.

It was my first lesson in the rewards of people-pleasing. If I denied my own needs and took care of others, I felt at least somewhat accepted. The real me had no value, in my mind. Truth had no value because telling it could spell abandonment. Maybe if I did everything right, she wouldn't leave me.

But no matter how hard I tried, I couldn't do everything right. When I tripped up, Mom would yell, "If people really knew who you are, they'd see what a phony you are!" But I guess, considering how much our whole family hid our true selves from the outside world, we were all phonies.

Kris was born when I was nine, and Mom was too sick and depressed at the time to take care of her new daughter. Suddenly, even more responsibility fell upon my shoulders.

When I would get out from under it all for a little while to take walks through the neighborhood, I usually had to take Kris with me in a stroller. But I was always trying to escape the craziness, so I'd sneak out of the house without Kris whenever I could. I paid a price for those glimpses of freedom, though. One day, I dared to take a walk without my sister, and when I got home, my mother was livid.

"Where were you?" she screamed. When I tried to answer, she screamed louder, "Shut up!"

"I just . . ."

"Shut up!" She picked up the nearest object and smashed it on the floor.

"I just want to tell you . . ."

"No excuses!" She picked up another object and smashed it.

I tried to get her to hear me. "I just . . . I'm sorry!"

But the more I tried to talk, the more out of control she became. As a little girl, I felt responsible for what she felt and expressed, and I wanted desperately for her to understand that I hadn't meant it.

Sometimes she'd whack me across the face with the back of her hand. "Your mouth!" Or she'd grab me by my hair and shake me hard.

Still, at other times, Mom could be kind and loving to me, especially when she wasn't depressed. I have a particularly fond memory from when I was in kindergarten. Mom came to my school and brought cookies for everyone. I was so proud. Another time, I wet my pants at school, and she came to pick me up. I was so embarrassed and scared that she would yell at me. Instead, she hugged and comforted me. I'll always remember that feeling of being safe in her arms. I knew in that moment that she really did love me, and I'd do anything to get more of that love.

Mom's mental illness came to a head when I was about 11. She was at a dinner function with my father when she just got up and left the restaurant. My dad was frantic because he had no idea where she'd gone.

Mom wandered the streets aimlessly until she found a church. Finally, the priest called my father. Shortly after, a police car pulled up to our house with Mom in the back seat. My grandparents were there, and everyone whispered, "Don't worry, Kathe. Your mom will be okay." But Mom just walked through the door of our house and didn't come out of her bedroom for days. Only my dad was allowed in. I pressed my ear up against the wall, trying desperately to hear something that would prove to me she was all right.

Eventually, I was allowed to go into her room. She was sitting in a rocking chair, looking out the window. She put me on her lap and held me. "It's okay, but I'm sick," she said. "You won't see me for a while. I need to be alone to get better." I was used to seeing her sick, so I took it to mean that she was physically ill again. But now I realize she was talking about her mental illness.

I cried and said, "It's okay. I understand you, Mom." I didn't really, but I felt it was my job to help her feel better.

It wasn't until I reached my early 20s that I found out my father was also mentally ill. After years of not understanding what was wrong with him, he was diagnosed with bipolar disorder.

A few years before that, however, when I was in my late teens, I found out that mental illness ran in his family. Dad and I were having a conversation and he said, as if he were reading a benign sports headline, "You know, my father hung himself."

"What?! My grandfather committed suicide?" I had never met my grandfather, but the image in my mind was horrific.

"Oh, sorry. I never told you that? I thought I did."

My mind whirled with this information. Would I become mentally ill too? If it ran on both sides of my family, what were the odds that I'd be okay? And would Dad try to kill himself like his father had?

One Sunday outing, we were all in the car together and Dad's arguing with Mom escalated until he stopped the car on some railroad tracks, refusing to move. I cried in the back seat while my mother and brother screamed, "You've got to get off the railroad tracks! Hurry! Move!"

"I don't give a shit!" was his answer. It was a power struggle, with the kids caught in the middle. Obviously he moved before a train came, but we were all terribly frightened. Maybe it was his suicidal impulses coming out in that moment.

I truly thought I was going to die that day, and as the tears streamed down my face, I vowed that if I lived, I would get far away from my parents as soon as possible.

These fights between Mom and Dad were terrifying to us children. Mom would put Dad down in front of us. "You're never home, and you leave me with *these kids*! Thanks for my miserable life!" So much for Cadillac Joe's ability to satisfy Chickie.

The shouting would escalate until the original reason for the argument was anybody's guess. Mom would lock herself in the bathroom or their bedroom.

"Okay, goddamn it!" he'd shout. "Do you want me to break down the fucking door? Is that what you want me to do? Is exploding the only way I can calm you down and shut you up?"

She would keep yelling until he'd actually put his fist through the door. My brother and I were always afraid he'd kill her—so much so that my brother often jumped between them and yelled, "Please stop! Don't hurt Mommy!"

It wasn't uncommon at this point for Mom to stop screaming and turn into a vulnerable little girl: "Please don't hurt me."

Once Dad walked right through the bathroom door like Herman Munster on that old TV series *The Munsters*. It was so absurd that they both started laughing. Then they kissed and made up, suddenly romantic with each other.

All of this was surreal and horrifying for my brother and me to witness. We couldn't possibly understand the nuances of a tumultuous adult relationship. While other kids were doing their homework or studying for a test, we were worrying that our father was going to murder our mother.

It's surprising, really, that Dad never hit Mom. But he often took it out on my brother, Joe. It wasn't in Dad's upbringing to hit a woman or a girl, but in his old-school thinking, it was something he could justify doing to his son. It started with Dad just smacking Joe on the butt, but it got worse over time.

Dad would back Joe up against a wall and shake him until his head was banging against the hard surface. It's amazing that Joe survived the abuse.

And when Dad was finished hitting my brother, he would look at me and shout, "Are you next?"

Luckily, he never hit me, but as much as I adored my father, that look traumatized me and haunts me to this day. I trembled with fear and begged for my life. "Daddy, I know. Daddy, I know. I know. I'm sorry. I'm sorry. Please!" Often I would run into the closet, hide under the bed, or lock myself in the bathroom until his rage was spent. If I could avoid doing or saying the "wrong" thing, maybe I'd stay safe, I thought. I had to quickly learn how to become what my parents needed me to be at any particular time. I had to gauge their mood and try to mold myself into the person they wanted me to be in that moment.

Still, as scary as my dad could be, this was love to me—sweet one minute and violent the next. I didn't know anything else.

And when Dad calmed down, he would always ask for forgiveness. He would cry with shame as he told me how much he loved me. He begged me to help him, but what could I do? I knew I couldn't turn to my grandmother or any other relative for help. That would have been violating the family secrecy.

Despite my father's sometimes-violent nature, my relationship with him was so different from my relationship with Mom. I was a daddy's girl. He doted on me whenever he could get away with it. Unfortunately, this set me up as a target of Mom's jealousy.

Because she wanted him all to herself, she attempted to keep us apart and we had to sneak time for long talks when she was asleep or not around. We talked openly about how crazy and demanding she was. Mom sensed that we were talking about her and feared that we were conspiring against her. Therefore, these talks were yet another secret I had to keep.

During our moments alone, Dad inspired me and gave me hope. "You can do anything you put your mind to," he'd say. When I was a little older, he drove me to rock concerts and waited in the car for me until the show was over. He would get up at midnight to pick me up when I was out with friends, and sometimes he'd slip me 50 bucks. "Don't tell your mother," he'd say. I didn't realize at the time that these seemingly sweet gestures of my dad's were yet another lesson in how to keep secrets for the people I loved. I believed that if you really loved someone, you'd do anything to protect that love, no matter how much you had to withhold from the outside world. No matter how much you had to hide yourself and the truth.

The biggest secret I kept, though, was the trauma and pain I experienced throughout my childhood. I hid that even from myself, and I closed the door to my heart in order to survive.

CHAPTER 3

SEARCHING FOR LOVE AND STABILITY

When I reached my preteen years, it was the time of Woodstock. The dawning of the Age of Aquarius, the self-help years, women's liberation, and Masters and Johnson. My mother read *I'm OK—You're OK*, the popular self-help book by Thomas Harris. The problem was that it gave her license to be as wacky as she wanted to be. Whatever she did was now "OK."

Luckily both Mom and Dad were a bit more stable by this time. Dad's business was doing well, and Mom's depression had eased somewhat with the help of prescriptions and therapy. They went into a kind of hippie phase—a culture that was magical to me. I loved the freedom and excitement of change all around me. Even today, I'd still wear long skirts and flowers in my hair if I could get away with it. But at the time, it became clearer than ever that my mom and dad made better friends than parents.

I knew they loved me in their way, but I felt invisible in their house. I just didn't feel that they were particularly interested in me. It was always so easy to get away with teenage behavior like staying out late or even all night. No one ever checked on me or enforced a curfew.

I would walk in the house in the morning as Dad headed off to work, saying I'd slept at my friend Nancy's house. He'd just smile and ask if I'd had a good time. Of course, little did they know that I was partying my ass off.

Lying to him made me feel empty inside, but when given free rein, a teenager is likely to push the limits. At the time, all I cared about was my freedom. So I started smoking cigarettes and pot and hanging out in the park after dark.

I could move seamlessly in and out of every group—the drug users, the jocks, the hippies, the nerds, the parents, and the teachers—and be friends with everyone. I had learned well in my bipolar household how to be a chameleon, molding myself into the person everyone needed me to be. This gift made me popular, but the real Kathe stayed hidden somewhere deep inside.

When I turned 18, I kept the promise I'd made to myself and left that house. It felt like making a prison break. I was finally free from the insanity and drama. But I was also completely lost and utterly unprepared for life as an adult. I had watched my "smart" friends applying for colleges and figuring out their majors. But Mom and Dad didn't offer much guidance when it came to planning my future, so what was I going to do to make my own way?

I wanted to go to college, but Mom and Dad couldn't afford the tuition. They also wouldn't fill out the necessary financial aid forms. "I'm not giving the government any info about our finances!" was my mother's response. Her secrecy habit was getting in the way of my plans.

One of my teachers had taken an interest in me and pushed me, but there wasn't much he could do without my parents' permission. If they didn't help me apply to schools, I couldn't go.

I wanted to be a nurse or an attorney—some profession that would allow me to help people—but my mother discouraged me from it. "Do something you enjoy," she said. "You're drawn to fashion, and you have a great sense of style. Why don't you become a buyer for a store?" So rather than going to a traditional four-year college, I went to the Fashion Institute of Technology (FIT) in New York City.

In the beginning, I was a fish out of water. I had been to the city for concerts and evenings out, but I was naïve about the world of fashion. I did have a sense of style, but I didn't know the top designers and didn't have the money to buy clothes with those kinds of labels. It was simply a different world, and I felt overwhelmed and inferior to the "princesses" from Long Island who felt everything from your makeup to your shoes had to be perfect. I sure wanted "in" with that group, though, and I was willing to do whatever it took to have what I perceived would be a better life.

After I'd spent about a year studying fashion, my friend Nancy decided to move to California, and I didn't want to be left behind. It was an opportunity to go to a real college, since state schools there were free. It also gave me a convenient excuse to break up with my boyfriend at the time, who I wasn't happy with.

But I didn't love California, and after being injured in a car accident there, I needed to fly back home to recover. I had no one to take care of me but my family. All of a sudden, they didn't seem so bad. I was 19, and all I wanted was my old life back.

But Mom had different plans. "You decided to go out on your own. Once you leave the house, you can't just come and go whenever you please. It's not a revolving door. I guess you'll just have to figure it out."

"Why can't I stay?" I pleaded with her. "My bedroom isn't even being used."

"Your father's business is going bankrupt, and our marriage is in trouble," she answered.

I thought she was being unfair. She allowed my brother, Joe, to come and go as he pleased, and to stay in the house periodically. It didn't seem to dawn on her that she should treat us equally. She played by her own set of rules.

Once again, I felt rejected and abandoned. How could she refuse to help her own daughter, especially after I'd taken care of her so often during my childhood? Why couldn't she extend herself for a short time until I could get back on my feet?

"Does Dad know I need to come back?"

She wouldn't answer. In retrospect, I realize that I should have defied her and spoken to him myself. But I was terrified of starting trouble. I began to wonder if maybe Mom was right—I was a problem. I had no direction, and I was wreaking havoc on their lives. I was filled with guilt and self-doubt.

Meanwhile, Mom led Dad to believe it was my choice not to move back in with them. "You know your daughter," Mom told him. "She's a free spirit, a wild child. She wants to be on her own."

It was another example of a secret that my mom kept to serve her own ends, even if it meant hurting me. There I was, 19 years old, battered and bruised from a car accident, with no job and no place to live. The only other person I could turn to was the boyfriend I'd left when I fled to California. So I went back to him. It seemed as though every choice I'd made up to that point had been the wrong one, so I figured it was best to just give up and settle for less.

He took me back, but reluctantly. He was angry that I'd left and was borderline abusive. I felt that by taking his abuse, I was paying for my sins, but I was also determined to find a way out.

Until I could get a job, I applied for welfare and food stamps. I had worked since I was 15 years old and had inherited my father's work ethic. But finding a job at 19 with only one year of college under my belt and little experience proved to be difficult. I was so embarrassed about taking welfare that I swore I'd never tell anyone— yet another shameful secret I felt I had to keep.

I made a promise to myself: *No more fuck-ups, Kathe! Get a grip on yourself. Nobody is going to take care of you but you.* I apologized to God for my sins and vowed to Him that I would get back on track. Before long, I managed to find housing on my own and left my boyfriend for good.

With the help of public assistance, I was also able to return to FIT part-time. Keeping my promise to God, I worked hard. It didn't take long for the professors and other students to take notice of how much I applied myself. I found out that I had a talent for marketing. People praised my ideas and projects.

One of my classmates knew I was looking for work and offered to help. "I have a friend who works in a showroom, and they're looking for a salesperson. She could probably get you a job."

To look the part for the interview, I borrowed a suit from a friend. It was winter, but I didn't own a decent coat. I just walked into the building without one.

The job was with a well-known hair accessories and sunglasses company that had a showroom on Fifth Avenue.

They carried accessories by designers like Anne Klein, Bill Blass, and Donna Karan. I didn't know what to expect, but the interview went well. Rose, the director of sales, took a liking to me; I have no idea why.

As I was leaving the interview, she asked, "Where's your coat?"

"Oh, I left it in the car." I think she could tell I was lying. I'm sure she realized I was embarrassed and really needed the job. Maybe she felt I was hungry enough that I would work hard. So she hired me and became my first mentor.

Accepting the job meant I had to quit FIT again. I was just a bit shy of my degree when I took the job with Rose, and I worked with her for nearly five years.

She groomed me, teaching me how to sell and how to speak with clients. She paid for me to have a complete makeover. This meant getting my hair cut and colored, a makeup lesson, and a manicure. She didn't buy me clothes, but she sent me to sample sales so I could get designer labels at low cost. She took me out to dinner and taught me the rudiments of fine dining, from what the different forks are for to where the water glass is placed. I felt like her Eliza Doolittle.

While I appreciated Rose immensely, she put me through hell with her impossible standards. She was always criticizing me, and I felt inadequate next to her. I would use Jersey slang, and she'd say, "Really, Kathe?" It was a challenge to win her approval, and I often went home in tears.

Yet by the time I was 20 years old, I had discovered that I did my best work under pressure. My experiences with Rose taught me that I could accomplish almost anything with hard work and determination. Eventually, I earned some accounts of my own, which allowed me to work with major retailers and some of the designers, like Donna Karan.

I went from working in the showroom to being promoted to marketing and advertising. I discovered that I had a talent for managing press shoots, selecting top models, and designing product packaging. People seemed to enjoy working with me as much as I enjoyed them. It was amazing to feel capable, self-sufficient, and successful for the first time in my life. I was off welfare and exploring the exciting city of New York, and I felt I had a sense of purpose. I had the apartment and the job. I was on my way!

Then, one fateful day when I was 23 years old, I ran into Dana, a friend from high school. She had been one of the "party girls" who was always cutting school, going to New York City, and using drugs. While I had been friendly with her and her group, I didn't spend a lot of time with that crowd.

Dana was trying to overcome her addiction to heroin and wanted me to help her. "I don't know much about drugs," I told her.

My experience had included smoking marijuana and snorting cocaine a few times. I guess I was lucky that none of my experimentation had led to addiction, so I didn't understand the power that drugs can have over addicts. I assumed anyone could get clean if they had enough willpower.

"I just need people in my life who are successful like you and don't do drugs," Dana said. I thought my friendship with her could offer me some excitement, and I was naïve enough to think I could help her.

One evening, she invited me to her apartment. "Do you remember Larry Crawford?" she asked.

"Of course, I do! I used to see him hanging out at the youth center with you." He was such a "hot" guy that I'd certainly noticed him. He was 24 years old and about 5 foot 11, with narrow hips like Mick Jagger's and a gorgeous head of long, dark-brown, shaggy hair like Rick Springfield's. Always dressed in tight jeans and a fitted T-shirt, he had a chiseled jaw, high cheekbones, the perfect nose, and the greenest eyes I'd ever seen. He was also witty. All the girls wanted to hang out with him.

He had always been part of the "cool bad boys" group. I had dated a guy from that circle, but once when he and his friends were planning a camping trip, I'd felt rejected because he refused to take me. "You don't belong with this group, and I'm not going to be the one to take you there." It was only later that I realized he wouldn't let me go because he didn't want to expose me to hard drugs.

Larry was already at Dana's apartment when I arrived. The two of them were like brother and sister.

"I'm really proud that I've been able to turn my life around," Larry told me. He'd come home for Thanksgiving after having moved to Seattle to get away from the drug scene and get clean. His older sister and her husband, who were hard-core addicts, had been responsible for getting Larry and his brother involved in drugs.

Dana talked me up to Larry. "Kathe's really got her shit together. She has her own apartment and a great job working in the city. Now that you've got it together and she's got it together, you two could be a good fit. You should ask her out."

Besides his looks, Larry was also enormously charming. He seemed so normal and different from the other guys I'd met. He knew a lot of what I called "stuff," from the best jazz bars to the coolest new bands to the latest coffee spot. He read like a sponge, and I was enamored with listening to him talk. Imagine, a guy I could actually learn from, who also found *me* interesting! I thought of him as a Renaissance man and, frankly, was in awe of him.

Yet, the red flags were lit up like neon. I knew getting involved with Larry was a risk and probably a huge mistake. But I was seduced by the possibility of having such an interesting man in my life. Could I finally have the love I'd been craving? Was it possible for me to find someone who'd take care of *me* for a change?

Despite my better judgment, I agreed to go out with Larry. We spent time at the jazz clubs on West End Avenue and Columbus Avenue in Manhattan. From the first night, I was just *with* him. We spent almost all of our time together—it was the proverbial whirlwind romance.

He had planned to return to Seattle, but he decided to stay with me instead. I was only 23, but I was already tired of dating, partying, and one-night stands. Someone wanted me for me, not what I could do for him, and that's all that mattered. I was weary of feeling alone. With Larry, I never felt alone.

In no time, we could finish each other's sentences. We laughed together, held hands, and kissed as we walked for hours in Central Park or went to fun events like the Big Apple Circus. We dreamed about traveling to Europe together and one day living in the Dakota, the building where John Lennon lived. We would go for days without answering the phone, just enveloped in each other.

We'd only been dating for a few months when Larry turned to me and said, "Let's move to Hawaii!"

I looked at him, surprised.

Then he said, "Let's get married!"

My breath stopped. I gazed into the eyes of this beautiful man and heard myself say, "Yes!"

I couldn't believe my ears. Had I really just said I'd marry him? After such a short time? I hardly knew him, and my gut was telling me to slow down.

But I closed my eyes and told myself, *It doesn't matter! He loves me. Do you hear that?* HE LOVES YOU, KATHE!

Freedom was calling us both.

So I became Kathe Crawford. We made our impulsive move to Hawaii with no jobs and just a little bit of wedding gift money from relatives. But I was on an adventure! I felt for the first time in my life that I was free to fly.

Of course, the move meant quitting my job with Rose. It was impulsive and crazy, and I wish I could tell you what I was thinking. But the truth is that I wasn't thinking at all. I was just madly in love. That little girl who had walked down the street mooning over the other families, wanting them to take her in, was going to create her *own* family! And I was going to do it right. No mess, like in my parents' house. I was going to be a free-spirited woman like Joni Mitchell.

Forget all that I had learned from Rose. Forget the success that I'd managed to create for myself. Forget the self-sufficiency that I'd finally achieved. I was willing to give it all up for this elusive love that I was sure I'd finally found.

Rose was absolutely furious, of course, and never forgave me for quitting. "Who is this guy? What's wrong with you?" she asked me. It was a legitimate question.

Yet I'd convinced myself that Larry was my ticket to happiness. I was on cloud nine, but Larry would soon become the heaviest anchor I'd ever have in my life, bringing me right back down to earth with a devastating thud.

CHAPTER 4

LIVING WITH MY CHOICES

My first year married to Larry was everything I'd dreamed it would be, but Hawaii wasn't what we'd dreamed at all. Jobs were given to people from the islands, not to transplants like us. We were unemployed, bored, and missing home.

What I didn't know then was that boredom is lethal for an addict. We'd spent a lot of our time partying, so even though Larry wasn't using drugs in Hawaii, he was still often high from drinking. Then I noticed that he was no longer satisfied with just a few drinks. At a pharmacy, he bought some cough medicine because it contained codeine even though he didn't have a cough. Still, I was too naïve to understand that he was struggling with his recovery.

When we finally returned to New Jersey, we were broke and had no place to live. My mother wouldn't let us move in, so we had to move in with Larry's parents. I was able to land a job pretty quickly, but not Larry. Once again, he had too much time on his hands and was stuck living with his mom and dad. I'm sure he felt like a failure.

Eventually we were able to get our own apartment. One night, I came home from work to find him with the strangest look on his face. It was an expression I hadn't seen before. As he held up a little packet of cellophane, I could literally feel his energy pull away from me and toward that drug. It was like I no longer existed. I knew in that moment, the dope would mean more to Larry than I did.

"You know I don't get high anymore," he began, "but I really, *really* want to get high tonight. I'm not sure why. I just feel like it. It's really no big deal. You've been with me night and day. I haven't been getting high, have I?"

He said it as though he deserved a "treat" after having been clean for a while. But I could tell he was lying. That look was his lying face—a look that would soon become all too familiar.

Yet, I was so stunned that I didn't say a word. And he interpreted my silence as consent.

Would he have thrown it away if I'd asked? Why didn't I say, "No! It *is* a big deal!"

The truth is, I knew that he'd already made up his mind whether I gave him my approval or not. I guess he wanted to share it with me so he wouldn't feel guilty about hiding it.

"Don't worry. I'm not going to start shooting dope all the time," he said. I wanted to believe him—so I did. I convinced myself that I was an open and understanding person and that I had such a great, honest relationship with my husband that it all would be okay.

I simply couldn't entertain the possibility of losing Larry, drugs or no drugs. I was deeply in love with him, and our relationship was just as deeply entrenched in my life. Even my parents loved him, which improved my relationship with them. He and my father drank beer together, swapped stories, and listened to Willie Nelson songs.

Of course, Mom and Dad had no idea my husband was a recovering drug addict. And now, right before my eyes, he was no longer recovering. He was an active junkie. I knew it, and Larry knew it. But we both kept up the pretense that we'd be fine. In that moment, we believed our survival depended on pretending.

It was so surreal to watch him cook the dope, draw it into the needle, and slide the needle into his arm. I could tell from the seductiveness that little packet of heroin had for him that our relationship would never be the same.

He looked at me and smiled. "It's so much better to be honest with you! You're amazing. I love you so much."

Larry's drug use was the first secret I would keep for him. My childhood had taught me well.

Larry and I got up the next morning and started our day just like every other day, both of us in strong denial about his drug use. Nevertheless, I was aware that our relationship was forever changed, and I carried a lot of fear about what the day would bring. I certainly felt betrayed, hurt, and taken advantage of.

When I was alone, I thought, *What have you done to your life, Kathe? If people find out about this, they'll know for sure that you're a fuck-up. And what if Larry keeps using? What kind of mess will you be in then? Saddled with a junkie. How did you let this happen?* I had portrayed Larry as a responsible man who would take good care of me, especially to my parents. If I admitted I'd made a mistake, I'd be humiliated.

I was torn apart because I loved this man deeply, and I had made a commitment to him that I didn't take lightly. I assured myself that I could keep him from using again without anyone ever finding out. Plus, if I left, what would I have and where would I go? I already knew my mother wouldn't allow me to come back home.

It was a while before I discovered Larry was still regularly getting high. Whenever I saw him preparing the drug, he would say, "It's no different from people who smoke a joint now and then. I'm just going to get high on the weekends."

He started out getting high about once a month, then a couple of times a month, then once a week, and then every two or three days. Sometimes he did speedballs, which were a dangerous combination of heroin and cocaine that's strong enough to kill you. He started hanging out with Dana, who had relapsed, and her friends again. I hated them and thought of them as a cancer that was destroying my life.

And with that, my worst fears became my reality. I had never dreamed that the word "junkie" would become such a big part of my life.

Surprisingly, Larry could function as an addict. He had gotten a construction job and managed to work hard all day while hiding his addiction. Then he'd either come home and sedate himself with beer or go out after work and get high. I didn't know which was worse—having him drunk at home, where I knew he was safe and could do no harm, or out somewhere dangerous so I didn't have to confront my vacant-eyed ghost of a husband sitting on the couch.

It got to the point where we barely interacted with each other, and before long, we didn't really have a marriage anymore. I guess you could say we were still friends. He hated hurting me, but the man I had married—the man with so many hopes and dreams for the future—was slipping away.

Every day, I'd close my eyes really tight and pray, "Don't let him walk in stoned. Please, not tonight! Let us have just one normal night. Meet friends, watch TV, and just savor our time together." But nights like that became more and more rare. I was losing my strength—and the battle. I was losing my husband to a chemical.

Whether he went out late at night or earlier in the day or evening, he'd lie about where he was going: "I'm just going out for a pack of cigarettes." "I'll just be gone a few minutes to pick up a loaf of bread." The lies were ridiculous, of course, and I wasn't fooled. Sometimes he'd return hours later with lame excuses. "Oh, I ran into Tom, and we got to talking." "I stopped by my mom's place."

"You're stoned!" I'd say to him.

"No, I'm not. I promise!"

"Larry, I'm not stupid. You might be able to get away with it at work, but I know you. I know exactly how you look and how you act when you're high. I'm not crazy. Just tell me you're stoned!"

"Why do you have to make me say it?"

"What, do you think not saying it means you aren't hurting me? You don't want to say it because it'll make you feel even worse about yourself. If that's true, then don't come home stoned, because I'm living with hurt and disappointment every single day! You hear me? You can't keep walking into this house high and then have a couple of beers and just crash into bed. I can't live like that!"

I wanted him to stop lying and tell the truth. The lying was worse than the drugs. Honesty between us was so important to me, particularly because there had been so much dishonesty in my childhood home. But because of the drugs, we had lost the truth in our relationship.

I felt like such a fool for getting stuck in this situation, and I hated myself for it. But I still didn't have the self-esteem, the resiliency, or the belief in my ability to create a life on my own.

Eventually, Larry's addiction escalated to the point where I would sometimes troll the streets of Harlem looking for him outside abandoned buildings that had become shooting galleries for junkies. When I'd find him, I'd plead with him to get in the car and I'd drive him home.

Other times, as hard as it is to admit even now, I drove Larry to Harlem to buy his dope. If I didn't drive him, he'd take my car and end up driving stoned. I was so worried he'd kill himself or someone else. When he went without me, I had to endure what felt like endless nights of not knowing if he'd overdosed, gotten killed for a bag of dope, or died wrecking his car.

During this time, my life was the darkest, loneliest place. I prayed every day that the nightmare would end and my world would fall back into place. But I hadn't encountered anything in my life more powerful than heroin.

Larry did try to get clean over and over and over. He'd manage it for short periods of time. He hated himself for what he'd become, and he begged me to help him. But my codependency was fully entrenched, because I believed him every time he'd say he'd straighten himself out. And I convinced myself that if I could just think of the right reason to make him stop, he would.

But whenever he did stop, it wasn't long before he started again. My life was always a shot away from falling apart.

Even though he asked for my help, he wouldn't listen when I dared to suggest Narcotics Anonymous or Alcoholics Anonymous meetings. He'd say, "I'm *not* a drug addict. Drug addicts live on the streets. They're criminals." To him, drugs were just something he did; they didn't define who he was. He knew he had a problem with them, but he wouldn't put himself in the same category as other addicts.

I guess you could say he had the attitude that he was better than a junkie. Classic denial.

Rehab wasn't a great option in the '80s, either. The facilities were more like psychiatric hospitals where you would detox and be released back onto the streets. Most people in those places had been forced to go there after an arrest. I'm sure there were better rehabs available if you had enough money to pay for them. We just didn't have the funds for something like that.

Eventually I talked him into trying a rehab, but not long after, he was using again.

And there I was through it all, holding his secret like I'd done for my parents. I had friends, but there was no one I felt I could confide in about something so shameful. It may have been primarily Larry's secret, but I couldn't help but assume that I'd lose every friend I had if they knew. I was terrified of anyone finding out, and I started to understand how my mother must have felt about hiding our family business.

Larry and I, along with his dealers and a few other drug users, were the only people who knew. Anything I felt about what I was going through was held inside me like a tornado of fear, pain, and worry. There was no opportunity to release any of these emotions, and I had no skills for dealing with them. I was on my own, so the feelings kept churning deep inside.

Then, a couple of years into the marriage, we found out I was pregnant. If I had been thinking straight, I would have used birth control. But I was young, and life was too chaotic to think straight. Plus, in the back of my mind, I thought a baby would finally get Larry to stop using. I wanted so much to believe that I could help us create the family we'd dreamed about. *Maybe if my will is strong enough*, I thought, *I can make it happen.*

"Larry, I'm having this baby. I *really* want this baby," I told him. "That means you're going to have to give up the drugs. You have to straighten up now. You just have to!"

"Okay, I know, I know. I'm going to stop," he said. But I could feel his anxiety about becoming a father. What drug addict would feel ready for such a thing, I suppose? You have a demon you can't control, and you know you can't be responsible for your own life, let alone a child's.

Still, I thought if he really tried, he could give up heroin just like someone could quit cigarettes. Larry wanted to believe the view through my rose-colored glasses, but unlike me, he understood the full power of his demons. He just wouldn't admit it to me—at least not yet.

Contrary to my best hopes, Larry's drug use got worse all through my pregnancy. He tried to play the role of a responsible husband and father-to-be, going to work all day. But then he'd get high and come home late. I waited and waited for him every night, not knowing what would walk through the door.

"It's got to stop, Larry. Please . . . Please, I'm begging you!" I said over and over.

And he'd say, "Tomorrow, tomorrow. I promise I won't get high tomorrow." He always promised, and I know he meant it in that moment. Sometimes he'd go as many as three days without shooting up, but by the fourth day, the heroin would call him back. I was in a constant state of disillusionment, fear, and dread.

Through it all, it was my baby who kept me going. In spite of everything, I wanted this child so much.

It was a May morning in 1983 at 6 A.M. when I went into labor, which was lucky because Larry hadn't left for work yet. He took me to the hospital and stayed there most of the day. We called our baby "Little Larry."

As the end of the day neared, though, I could tell my husband was worried he wouldn't be able to make it through the night without a fix, even though he didn't have the heart to say it. "I'm going to go home and get a couple of things," he said. But I knew what he was really going to do. I felt crushed as I watched him walk out the door of my hospital room, leaving his newborn son behind, and I couldn't imagine that the hurt I felt could ever heal.

"I'm going to raise this baby with or without Larry," I said to myself. Despite the chaos of my life, when I held my son in my arms and looked into his eyes, all I felt was pure bliss. I had a respite from the disillusionment and fear. The love I felt for him immediately was so unconditional, so all-encompassing.

I thought of my mother and wondered if she had ever felt such unconditional love for me. *She loved me, but not like this*, I thought. It became even clearer to me that my childhood hadn't been "normal," and I resolved that I would *never* allow my child to feel the way I had when I was growing up.

This love I felt for my baby was the purest I'd ever experienced. I hadn't even been aware that a love like this was possible. It was beyond what I felt for my husband, which was enormous, but still romantic love.

So, my son taught me how to love. It saddened me to acknowledge that he was born to such imperfect parents. I knew all too well what that was like, and it was the last thing I wanted for my kid. I vowed to love and protect him as much as and as best I could, even if it meant dying for him.

I still hoped and prayed that the baby would help Larry get clean, but the prospect of being a father only seemed to make his addiction worse. His fears and insecurities overwhelmed him, and he started to get high twice a day sometimes. "Why would you rather shoot dope than come home to us?" I asked him. But he had no answer for me.

I couldn't let him hold Little Larry when he was high. And he was always high. So I finally got desperate enough to force him to make a choice. It was no longer just about me. Every moral value I'd ever had resurfaced and shifted me inside. I had to do the right thing.

"I won't do this anymore," I told Larry. "It's us or the drugs. You either have to get clean, or you have to leave."

He looked at me as though he'd seen this coming.

"I can't stop," he said. Then he paused. "I'm not ready to stop . . . and . . . and I'm too afraid to stop," he continued. "So it's better for you both that I leave." I'd never heard more heartbreaking words in my life.

"You knew this was a risk. You should never have married me. I can't do this to you or my son. You deserve so much better. I know I'm a loser, and I'm not going to drag you down with me."

It may sound strange, but in that moment, I could see a glimpse of the man I'd fallen in love with. He was a good man with a bad addiction. He left because he didn't want to hurt us anymore. My anger would come back soon enough, but I couldn't feel hatred toward or want revenge against him. My heart broke for this man who was giving up everything he'd truly wanted for a chemical. It was tragic.

But for the safety of my son, I had to be willing to say good-bye and hand the man I loved over to his demons. The demons, quite simply, had won.

Of course, I was terrified about being left to raise our son alone. "What's going to happen?" I asked Larry. "I don't know what to do! I don't know what's going to happen."

"I don't know what's going to happen either," Larry said.

When he walked out the door, I wanted to crumble. I didn't know if I'd ever see him again. I didn't know how long he'd survive. As he left, I watched him through the window with the tears streaming down my face and Little Larry in my arms. I tried to memorize the way my husband looked as he got into a friend's car without ever looking back at us.

I knew that the first thing he would do was get high.

I also knew it was better for my son and for me that Larry had left. But I couldn't help but feel devastated and abandoned. There I was, alone with my six-month-old baby. I didn't have a job anymore. I had no money or prospects for getting a job. Exhausted, I lay down on the bed and held Little Larry in my arms for a long time. That's when I made a promise to him and to myself. I looked down at Little Larry, so tiny and innocent. He had no idea of the turmoil he'd been born into. "You won't remember this moment, but I will. I'm making you a promise for life that I'll always take care of you and love you unconditionally, no matter what. You'll never have to settle for crumbs like I did. Your life will be filled with love. I'm giving you all of me—my heart, my soul, every piece of myself that I have to give. It's me and you."

Then, I had another conversation, this time with God. It was a very spiritual moment for me. "God, I'm asking you to help me because it's all up to me now, and I will *not* let my son down. I can't, and I won't." You know how little kids have imaginary friends? Well, God was like my imaginary friend. I didn't have to keep secrets from God because He already knew everything. He was the witness to the promise I made to my son, and that promise gave me the strength to go on.

Certainly, after all that had happened to me, parts of my heart had closed, but Little Larry kept parts of it open for me. He was the light. I couldn't let myself wallow or fall apart. I had a purpose—a reason to keep getting up in the morning.

Nevertheless, the harsh reality was that I didn't have money for food or rent. I couldn't even afford a babysitter so I could look for a job. I didn't want to go to my parents for help, but I couldn't think of anywhere else to turn, even though I knew full well they might say no again.

That was the first time I shared Larry's secret. I felt I had no choice but to disclose his addiction to my parents. My fears were well founded, because just as my mother had turned me away a few years earlier, this time she said, "You've made your bed, and now you've got to lie in it."

"But, Mom, I have a baby now, and I don't have a job to pay the rent! He's your grandson! Can't I come home for just a little while until I can get money coming in?" I felt so ashamed. I had married a drug addict, was now alone with a baby, and had no job. What had I become?

"Absolutely not! I can't handle your problems. I have my own."

I started to sob. "I don't know what to do. I don't have any options left! I have to go back to work, and who will watch the baby then?"

It stung like hell. She knew how much I loved my son, and I just couldn't understand how my mother could turn away her own daughter and grandchild, considering our desperate situation. Did she love me? Did Larry?

My grandmother did help me out a bit financially, but she didn't offer to take me in. I understood why. She was afraid of the drugs. She could see the fear in me after what I'd experienced.

Then I thought of Larry's mother. She was compassionate, buying diapers and clothes for the baby and cooking food for us, but she was already taking care of her daughter's two children because her daughter was also an addict. "Why won't your parents help you?" she asked me.

Oddly, the humiliation of all the rejections gave me the strength to keep going. The next day, I applied for government assistance. Then I set about finding a job, asking my sister or a friend to watch Little Larry for an hour or so while I went to interviews.

The first job I got was such a blessing, because my boss was enormously kind to me at a time when I needed it most. In order to go to work, however, I needed a day-care center. The cost was $475 a month, which was more than I could afford combined with the rent I was paying.

So I moved out of the apartment I had shared with Larry—the home where I thought we'd live happily ever after—and found a cheaper place that included heat in the rent. Unfortunately, the landlord would shut the heat off at night to save money, which gave Little Larry a terrible croupy cough. For a while, doctors even thought he might have cystic fibrosis.

The thought of leaving my baby with strangers at the day care added to my anxiety and worry, but at the same time, it was peaceful not worrying about Larry coming home high. I could rest in the pure joy of my son. We cuddled in bed together while I read to him. We shared a bond that none of my life's challenges could touch.

The government paid for Little Larry's formula and some dairy products. That was it. Even though I was grateful for the assistance we got, at the end of the month, no matter how much I juggled, the numbers just didn't add up. I ate a lot of peanut butter during that time, and my cupboards were filled with those boxes of awful macaroni and cheese.

Our financial situation meant I still couldn't leave Larry's ugly drug world behind entirely. I found out that he was still working, and on Fridays I would drive over the George Washington Bridge to 125th Street in Harlem, where I had taken him to buy his drugs. I had to catch him before he spent all of his pay on heroin.

My sweet neighbor babysat Little Larry when I made my weekly drives to Harlem. She was the only person outside of my family who knew that Larry had left us, although she didn't know he was a drug addict. She just knew that I was struggling. My fear was that she would close the drapes and ignore me if she knew the truth.

Every time I crossed the George Washington Bridge and drove into Harlem, a crime-ridden area at the time, my heart raced. What would happen to Little Larry if I got raped or shot? But I felt hopeless enough to take the chance, because I couldn't think of any other way to take care of my son.

The first time I saw my husband on the streets after he walked away from our home on that day when I thought I might never see him again, he wouldn't look me in the eyes. He couldn't face me. While I was relieved to see that he was still alive, I no longer felt the connection between us. Obviously he was going downhill fast. Whatever hope I'd held on to that we might be able to reconcile was shattered. But I fought back the tears and kept my focus on getting the money I needed to care for my child.

Larry wasn't living anywhere; he simply surfed the couches of friends and probably passed out on the floor of one of the shooting galleries most nights.

I'd drive to the corners where I knew he hung out, and I'd swallow my fears as I approached some of his junkie friends. "Which gallery is Larry in? Have you seen him?" I'd sit parked outside the one they indicated, waiting for him to come out.

As soon as I saw him, I'd jump out of the car and yell, "Lar! Lar!"

"Oh, yeah, I forgot," Larry would say, handing me a few bucks as he walked away. I'd look into his hollowed eyes. He had become painfully thin, and his cheeks were sunken. Every time I saw him, he seemed to have moved further away from us. In that state, Little Larry and I didn't matter to him. Had he ever known me? Had I ever known him? My heart broke a little more each week.

One night, I had to wait so long for him that I entered the shooting gallery to look for him. It was like stepping into hell—beyond anything I had been capable of imagining. Worse than any movies I'd seen. If someone had walked in with horns, a tail, and a pitchfork, I wouldn't have been surprised. The place was filthy, with bottle caps and dirty needles lying on the floor. It smelled of booze and what I could only characterize as death. Junkies were all over the floor in varying states of consciousness, many with needles still in their arms. Some of them were probably dead. Perhaps they'd overdosed, or they were just so high that they appeared dead. Some of the ones who were still conscious came up to me, pulled at me, tried to touch me, and begged me for money.

Once I found Larry in the gallery, seeing him in that place was more than I could bear. He'd officially become the kind of addict he despised—the type he'd always considered himself better than. But he couldn't deny it any longer. He was now a true, die-hard junkie.

I winced and ran out of there as fast as I could. He followed me outside and gave me some money, trying to convince me once again that he would straighten himself out. "Everything will be okay," he said. But I never went back inside one of those shooting galleries again. No matter how desperate I became, it had been too traumatic for me to ever repeat the experience.

Trying to find my junkie husband to get money to take care of my kid was just about the worst thing I had ever had to do. I felt like I was selling my soul. I was living in two worlds—the loving cocoon I was trying to create with my son and the dreadful hell of junkies with arms swollen like Popeye's from shooting up. The kind of people who would steal anything from you.

Until I could make enough money on my own, however, I couldn't see a way to make the break from Larry entirely.

In spite of all of this ugliness, I was determined that my son's life would be filled with joy. From my point of view, that included keeping his father's secret. If people had known, how would they have treated us? I didn't want the other day-care parents to be afraid of my kid. Not allowing people to find out about Larry's addiction became a way to protect not just Larry, but also our son.

When I picked Little Larry up at day care at the end of each day, we wouldn't go home for dinner right away. Instead, I'd take him to the park. I'd place him in a swing and give him a gentle push. We'd dig in the sandbox. Sometimes we'd go to the library and look at books together, or I'd take him to a nature center. I'd find all the free, fun things for a child and parent to do. It was our precious time together, and I was trying hard to rebuild my life.

My son brought me so much happiness. His face lit up when he saw me, and he asked me endless questions. Whenever someone else was around, he didn't want to share me with them.

When Little Larry was about 18 months old, Larry got arrested for drug possession and landed in the county jail for a month. I'd managed to become a bit more financially stable by then, and I vowed I would never go see Larry in jail. But his mother pleaded with me to go. I also swore I wouldn't take the baby to see him, but she said, "If Larry sees the baby, it'll help him."

As I sat at the jail with all the other women holding children on their laps while they waited to see the fathers, I wanted to vomit. This wasn't the person I wanted to be. This wasn't the person I ever thought I'd be.

When we were taken to see Larry, he looked at us in horror. "I can't believe you're here! You should have known better than to come here! I don't want you to see me like this. And you brought the baby?"

Surprisingly, though, jail turned out to be a blessing for my husband. It was his rock bottom—the turning point that made him finally want to get real help. I told my parents about the situation, and this time, they agreed to help. It was a huge surprise, and I was happy to accept their assistance because we needed it so desperately. I was stunned when Mom offered to research rehabs and found a new one for Larry to try. "I'm going to help you get back on your feet," she said.

When Larry was released from rehab, he no longer had a job. So my father took him to a construction site one day and showed him the ropes. Since Larry was smart and had some construction experience, he was able to acquire the skills quickly. Soon, he discovered a whole host of talents he'd never known he had.

We started spending time together now and then, testing the waters, and eventually Larry asked if he could come home. Naturally, I was reluctant. Even though we didn't have much money, Little Larry and I had created a happy life for ourselves. I didn't want to upset what we had, and my gut said *no!*

I still loved my husband, but I didn't trust him or know if I ever could. When Larry was clean, he was the man I'd fallen in love with, and that man was good and kind. But when he was using drugs, he turned into someone else, and Little Larry was getting old enough to emulate the adults around him and ask difficult questions.

"If you move back in, how do I know it won't happen again?" I asked. "How can I trust you after everything you've put me though? You'd have to stay clean this time, Larry. I mean it. Otherwise, you're out of here."

"I know. I get it. I really want this now."

"Little Larry's getting older and will absorb everything he sees. I won't allow any junkies in our lives ever again. They can't be around us at all. You understand that, right?"

"Yes, I really want to stay clean, and I don't want to see those people anymore. It's too dangerous. If I see them, it's too easy to start using again, and I really don't want to go back there. But I can't get straight unless I'm with you. I *need* you."

That was such heavy guilt to lay on me. If I truly had that power, I could help him change his life. If I didn't, I'd end up heading down that same awful road again. As scared as I was, I also knew that if I turned Larry away, he would end up back on the streets. So in spite of my better judgment, I took a deep breath and let him move into our cold apartment with us. Our broken family was finally piecing itself together again.

Terror churned just under the surface in every cell of my body. But I had to hope that we could rewrite our story this time.

In what felt like no time, Larry had mastered carpentry skills and learned how to mold and fabricate gorgeous copper trims and how to create beautiful custom homes. He truly was a talented and hardworking man who was no longer just working at a "job." He had a profession, a real career, and he was able to provide for us financially. It gave him a new focus that kept him occupied doing work that he excelled at and enjoyed. For the first time in a long time, my husband felt useful, normal, and hopeful. That allowed me to feel hopeful too. Was "normalcy" truly a possibility for us? I wanted it more than I'd ever wanted anything, and I started to fall deeply in love with my husband again.

Eventually Larry's talents advanced to such a degree that he was able to start his own business. He loved it, and people admired him for it. He found beauty and purpose in how he made his living, and I'm sure this helped him stay clean, maybe even more than our little family did.

Larry also developed a love of fishing and would get up at five in the morning to go out on the water, sometimes with my dad. I'm sure it was meditative and peaceful for both of them.

But despite my insistence that he stay away from them, Larry was still occasionally in contact with the junkies he had known. Many of his old friends wanted him to hire them so they could work and make money too. "We've been friends for years," they'd say. "Come on, help us out. We need a break like you had to get clean. Who's going to help us?" They laid guilt trips on him, and he got sucked in a couple of times. But predictably, every time he tried to hire any of them, it was a nightmare. And every time one of those people came around, my fears came right back up to the surface like bile.

"Larry, you can't hire these people or be around them. I know you want to help them, but you've got to think of yourself and of us now." He understood that hiring them would be a slippery slope to destruction, so he stopped doing it. I know it took a lot of strength on his part to say no to his friends, and I was proud of him for it. By refusing them, he showed me how much he wanted our life together to work out.

Yet, even while Larry stayed clean, some habits were hard to break. He continued to drink beer and smoke cigarettes. He was the kind of guy who could come home from work, play with Little Larry, and finish a six-pack without becoming visibly drunk. Of course, it bothered me and kept our relationship always on the edge. I knew it wouldn't take much for him to start using drugs again. Then, all would be lost.

Nevertheless, I was afraid to tell him what I was feeling. Would my complaints be exactly what put him over the edge? So I kept my worries to myself for a long time—they were a knot of fear buried inside me.

One minute, I'd allow myself to be open to the happiness of being with the husband and child I loved so deeply. The next moment, I'd be scared to death about what might happen next. It was like standing on a cliff, just praying that Larry wouldn't slip off the side and pull Little Larry and me along with him, bouncing off the rocks.

I would be in hell again if Larry left, but I was already in a sort of hell with him at home, because I didn't know if or when the bottom would drop out of his sobriety. Would he go out to use again one night, overdose, get killed, or never come back? I felt I had no control over my life, but I held on tight, trying to control as much of it as I could.

CHAPTER 5

THE MAKING OF THE ULTIMATE SECRET

By 1987, Little Larry was four years old, and Larry had been clean for a year and a half. It was something of a miracle, and I could almost tell myself that our lives were falling into place. *Almost.*

I was reluctant to take a chance or plan ahead, but there were two urges I couldn't resist—my commitment to my son to provide him with a normal life, which meant a house complete with a backyard, and a strong yearning for another baby. Both were huge financial risks, and having another child was probably downright reckless and selfish. But when you're young and your heart wants something so much, you convince yourself the risks aren't as great as you think. You take a deep breath and tell yourself you deserve it.

So I found a house that we could afford (barely) in a safe, working-class neighborhood in northern New Jersey, less than an hour outside of New York City.

My parents were doing better financially, so they surprised me by generously agreeing to loan us money for the down payment. There was no time for us to save enough money, and I felt I couldn't wait any longer.

For us, there would be no more crummy little apartments where the heat was shut off in the middle of the night. I was almost 30, and I was determined to have something we could call our own.

That was me. I would set my strategy, pull all of my resources together, and focus my efforts. I was the visionary of the family who could make lemonade from lemons. The doer who brought the glue.

I loved our neighborhood and our one-lane road right from the start. It had charm and character. It symbolized, for me, just the kind of stability and peace I'd wanted for as long as I could remember. And now maybe—just maybe—I had it. A place we could call home in a quaint little 1930s-era ranch house on a street called Pocahontas Path.

The house was pale yellow with baby-blue shutters. It wasn't quite 1,500 square feet, and it had faded aluminum siding. There was no garage. But it was a fixer-upper with lots of potential, so I bought it before I showed it to Larry.

Then, after getting over a heartbreaking failed pregnancy, I managed to become pregnant again. It seemed as though we'd just moved into the house when our second son, Brian, was born in 1988.

There was no question that my sons took up the most real estate in my heart. As scary as it was to be a mom, it was the biggest blessing for me in the midst of all the worry about my husband.

We certainly didn't have a perfect life, but it felt like we were on the upswing. I couldn't help but hope that we could finally have the kind of normal life I'd always dreamed of. It was right there within my grasp. I could taste it!

Larry wasn't using drugs, and he worked hard in a profession that gave him a lot of satisfaction. And I had my two beautiful boys. We were growing roots, and I was about as settled as I'd ever felt in my life. I finally owned a piece of the American dream, and if I pushed the fear down far enough, I could just about believe that I was a princess living in her happily-ever-after moment.

But we still had the down payment to pay back to my parents, the mortgage to pay off, and two little kids to care for. That's why I made sure we both applied for life insurance. Just in case. Because you never know.

Our last normal day was after nearly two years in our new house. Larry was at work, and Little Larry was at kindergarten. I was home alone, holding Brian in my arms. The phone rang, and I rushed into our dated country-style kitchen to answer the call. As I ran into the room, I pictured how it would look after we renovated it. *There's plenty of time for that*, I thought.

It was our insurance agent. "Larry's life insurance policy has been denied," he said.

My heart immediately sank. I instantly felt in my bones that our happy little life on Pocahontas Path was in jeopardy.

"Why?" My throat tightened as I braced myself for his answer.

"I don't know," he replied. "Legally, they can't release information like that to me, but in my experience, with someone Larry's age, the reason is usually medical. The only person who can give you the results of your blood test is a doctor, so you'll need to get to one right away."

We didn't have a family doctor, so I spent the next few days trying to locate one who would see us quickly. Larry didn't seem to be worried, but that was Larry. Despite everything he'd been through, he could stay relaxed and laid back. I used to think it was his strength, but I came to understand that it was his coping mechanism—the powerful denial capabilities of an addict.

I, on the other hand, was the opposite of laid back. My worst fears immediately took over. Every day that I didn't know why he'd been denied life insurance, my nerves frayed a little more. I needed an answer to ease the chaotic swirl of fearful thoughts in my mind.

When we finally got to the doctor's office, the doctor wasn't very friendly. Actually, that's an understatement. He barely looked at us as we sat down across from him. Instead, he focused on Larry's file. There were no pleasantries, no exam, and no hint of the Hippocratic oath. He just read us the results of Larry's battery of tests without the decency of even trying to hide his lack of compassion.

"Your blood work shows that you have AIDS," he said. "There's really nothing we can do for you. There's no cure, and there's no treatment. The best advice I can give you is, if you have kids, go home and hold them tight. Keep your family and friends close, and get your life in order because you're going to die."

We sat there speechless. Larry hunched over and dropped his face into his hands.

I looked at my husband. I looked at the doctor. Time seemed to stop. What had he said?

I crumpled over into my lap.

When I looked at Larry again, I saw that his laid-back persona had been destroyed. I couldn't imagine what it was like for him to hear such a thing, and I was suddenly aware of the fragility of his body. He would never be the same. Nothing would ever be the same. And oh, dear God, our beautiful little boys!

The doctor wasn't remotely interested in comforting us or answering any questions. Before we had a chance to fathom what we'd just been told, we were ushered out of his office.

Moving in slow motion, we made our way back to the parking lot and climbed inside our old Volvo. We sat there stunned, unable to make eye contact as we tried to absorb the news. My heart felt like it was exploding, and I wanted to roll down the window and throw up. *AIDS? Larry was going to die?*

But wait! Did I have AIDS too? Was I going to die? Would our sons be orphans? Who would take care of them? My mind couldn't make sense of it.

After a few moments of sitting in the car, the harsh reality hit Larry, and he finally broke down. His shoulders heaved, and waterfalls of tears poured from his eyes. The image of this man I loved so deeply trying to come to terms with a death sentence will forever stay imprinted on my heart.

We were in free fall, and like Humpty Dumpty, we wouldn't be able to put the pieces back together again. We sat there and cried together for the life we'd thought we would have. A life that, with this news, was already dead.

I loved him so much, but I also hated him in that moment. Yes, Larry was going to die, and that was awful. But he was also a junkie—a criminal. A selfish and careless man who had destroyed our lives with dirty heroin needles.

Maybe the smartest thing I could have done in that moment was to run! Run as fast as I could to protect myself and my boys. Who would have blamed me for leaving? I had my kids to think about and protect, after all.

But at the same time, I couldn't think of leaving him. Who would take care of him and love him as I could? If I left, he'd surely die on the streets as just another junkie. He was my husband and the father of my children. So no, I'd never leave him—not ever.

As the tears streamed down my face, I looked at this terrified man, and our eyes finally met, though no words passed between us.

Then, in one split second, we both had the same realization that if I'd gotten AIDS from Larry, our new baby could have contracted it from me! And Little Larry could have contracted it too! The thought was unbearable, so we just held each other tight.

"We'll figure this out together," I told him. "We'll do whatever it takes. I won't let you die! That doctor was such a bastard. How dare he tell us there's nothing we can do. Of course there is, and together, we'll find the answers. I promise you, Larry!"

I wished we could have more time to talk, to comfort one another, and to hold each other. But we had to get back home to the kids. My mother was watching them and would expect us soon.

As I started the car, Larry said one last thing to me. "Until we figure this out, please don't tell anyone."

And like the good little secret-keeper I'd grown to be, I said, "Of course not. I'll never tell anyone. I would never do that to you or to us."

By 1987, Rock Hudson had already died of AIDS, and the medical profession was frantically trying to understand the disease. Most doctors still knew very little about it. Case in point: the doctor we saw had told us that Larry had AIDS when he really should have said that Larry was HIV-positive. The medical community didn't yet understand even the stages of infection with the virus.

Most people already had full-blown AIDS by the time they were diagnosed, so they were dead within a year. The streets outside of St. Vincent's Hospital in New York's Greenwich Village were lined with the sick and dying. It was ground zero.

Sadly, a lack of medical understanding wasn't the worst experience we were getting ready to face. We'd seen enough news coverage to know that many people thought of HIV/AIDS as a plague in people they deemed the "outcasts" of society—homosexuals, drug addicts, and derelicts.

Even in cases of innocent infected children, fear and prejudice ran rampant. There had been big headlines about Ryan White, a 13-year-old boy who had been forced out of school because he had HIV. I saw him on Oprah's TV show, talking about how he had contracted the virus from a blood transfusion given as treatment for his hemophilia. Donated blood wasn't tested for HIV back then, and it clearly wasn't his fault that he'd been infected. He was just a kid who wanted to live as normally as possible after his diagnosis. Doctors were certain it was safe for him to be around other students, but people were still afraid to trust doctors' assurances that the disease couldn't be contracted through casual contact. They didn't want to touch people with HIV or even be in the same room with them. So parents protested and demanded that Ryan leave.

It was terrifying. Brian was only three months old! If sweet, young Ryan White had become alienated and an outcast because of his disease, imagine what people in our small community would think of Larry, of me, and of our kids. The doctor hadn't even been able to muster an ounce of empathy, so how could we expect it from anyone else?

We knew that the first thing people would want to know was "How did he get it?" And that question would open up another box of secrets that would have made

Pandora gasp. I was so accustomed to covering for my husband, and what could be more intimate or private than a diagnosis of AIDS?

So my promise to him flowed right out of my mouth. There was no need to take the time to make a "decision" or wonder about consequences. Keeping secrets was how I'd been taught to live, and I never thought to question it. As far as I was concerned, I was a lion protecting her cubs.

After Larry's diagnosis, it took every ounce of strength we had to make our daily lives look as though nothing had changed. But behind closed doors, our lives were turned upside down, and we didn't know what else to do but continue with our usual routines.

Those routines were just about the only comfort we could find. Plus, sticking to our day-to-day responsibilities allowed us to deny the truth and keep up the pretense with the boys and our families, friends, co-workers, and neighbors. We had to perform the roles of people who had it all together, and staying busy allowed us to stay enough ahead of our terror to function.

I was in shock, drowning in pain and filled with uncertainty. I cried constantly when no one was around, but I wouldn't allow Larry or the boys to see me break down.

I would drop my gaze when Larry walked through the door after work, and I fought back the tears when I watched him playing with our sons. In my mind's eye, I couldn't help but see myself without Larry not far in the future. It was unbearable. I missed him already, even though he was still there. Everything I did felt so final.

But my main concern during the first few days was finding out if my boys were going to be okay. I had to get them to the pediatrician right away, I had to get myself tested, and I had to find a doctor for Larry who would actually treat him rather than just send him home with a death sentence. So while Larry was at work during the day, it fell to me to take care of these tasks. On the phone to doctors and clinics, I struggled to say, "My husband has been diagnosed with AIDS. Can you help me?" And every day, I'd hear the same answer on the other end of the line: "I'm sorry, but there's no cure. No hope."

Of course, in order to get advice about the kids, I had to disclose our secret to our pediatrician. He was stunned. He told me he'd seen some AIDS babies whose mothers were addicts. He said the babies were being abandoned by their mothers, and no one would adopt them.

But luckily, he felt that Brian showed no signs of being infected, and that he was too young to be tested. He also thought it was best to avoid testing Little Larry unless we had real evidence that he'd been infected.

"Look, once someone is diagnosed with HIV, it goes on the record forever," the doctor told me. "Brian and Little Larry would be flagged in just about everything, and so would you." Larry's life insurance policy denial was a case in point.

"Get yourself tested at a clinic," the pediatrician went on. "They'll identify you by a number and keep you anonymous. If you come back negative, the chances are that Brian doesn't have it, either."

In those days, it took two to three weeks to get your results. To say I was terrified during that time is a ridiculous understatement. It was an unfathomable amount of fear. I would sit nursing Brian, not even knowing if I should be. The pediatrician had said it should be fine, but I still worried that I could be infecting him. The loving act of giving my baby a healthy start turned into anguish and worry.

My mind raced with worst-case scenarios. How long would Larry live? Would he suffer? How long would my boys have a father? Would they be traumatized by what they saw their father endure? What would our lives be like after Larry died? What would happen to the boys if I had HIV too? Was my sweet baby boy going to die? If I had contracted it and passed it on to Brian, what would happen to Little Larry? Would he be the sole survivor of our family? Or could Little Larry have contracted it somehow from his dad by drinking from a contaminated cup?

Then there were the financial worries. How would the boys and I survive without a life insurance policy on Larry? What if we couldn't get medical insurance for him once my COBRA coverage ran out in a few months? How was I going to pay our mortgage without Larry's income? How would I pay for the medical bills, day care, sneakers, food, and college tuition?

I wanted to call someone—anyone—and talk about it, but I wouldn't break my promise to Larry. What if the person I chose to tell turned away from us? What if that person spread the secret to others? I just couldn't risk it.

And so it was that my husband was infected with a deadly virus, and I was infected with another secret.

CHAPTER 6

THE BURDEN OF SECRET-KEEPING

When my test results came back negative for the virus, I was overcome with relief. It was the first time in almost a month that a little bit of good news had crossed my path. This meant that the likelihood of Brian or Little Larry having the disease was slim.

Larry and I hugged and cried together in celebration. But, of course, our celebration was short. Larry was still going to die.

Even with my test results, we couldn't be 100 percent certain that either of our sons would be okay. I tried to remember if Larry had ever cut himself while playing with the boys or while changing Brian's diaper. Larry worked with metals, so his hands frequently had cuts on them—cuts that it had never dawned on us could be harmful to anyone else. I hadn't yet learned exactly how HIV was transmitted, so I watched my kids like a hawk. I was paranoid that they could still contract the virus, and I looked every day for the slightest hint of a symptom.

Little Larry would ask, "Daddy, can I have a sip of your iced tea?"

"Oh, no, honey!" I'd say as I quickly jumped up and grabbed the glass. "Daddy could have a cold or something, and you don't want to get his germs." I probably got a reputation as a germophobe with anyone who witnessed my behavior.

When Brian turned one, our pediatrician repeated his recommendation that, like Little Larry, we not put Brian through a test unless he became symptomatic. He hadn't seen many cases of HIV in infants, even though the number of newborns with the virus was growing. He didn't think Brian or Little Larry showed any telltale signs, so as tough as it was, we did as he advised.

We had known our pediatrician for many years, and he was one of those old-fashioned salt-of-the-earth doctors you rarely find anymore. I knew he cared about my children, and Larry and I had to trust someone, because how were we to know what was best?

Unfortunately, most members of the medical community weren't helpful to us at all. This was before the Internet, so you couldn't just google names of facilities that worked with HIV patients. I had to do some very discreet investigating to find out where we could get assistance. Organizations like Project Inform in San Francisco and the Gay Men's Health Crisis (GMHC) in New York were true advocates for those with HIV/AIDS. We were so lucky to have them. They funded research, and they provided care and counseling. Most importantly, they demanded action from the government and drug companies, all of whom had turned their backs on the disease and the patients who had it.

Still, I felt I had to be careful not to put us on mailing lists in case a bit of our mail ended up in the hands of a neighbor. It wasn't like much of the heterosexual community was making donations to GMHC at that time, so I didn't know how I would explain getting mail from them.

At first, GMHC referred us to meth clinics and rehab centers for drug addicts, but those resources proved to be of absolutely no help. It was as if they felt "What's the point in trying to save a drug addict? They'll just go out and use again anyway." We went back to GMHC asking for doctors, and they gave us some names and informed us about clinical trials.

They also taught us about safe sex. Surprisingly, the physical intimacy between the two of us increased. It was very important to me that Larry never feel he was untouchable or unworthy of love because of his HIV. We took every precaution and connected intimately not just with our bodies, but with our minds and spirits. Our kisses held so much love, as we no longer took our precious time together for granted.

The people in the organization were extraordinarily kind to me. I'll always remember them with immense gratitude. I can't say I developed a personal friendship with anyone there, but it was a relief that someone genuinely cared and understood what we were going through. Whenever I felt like I was falling apart, I could call them, and they would talk me off the ledge. Yes, I was talking to a stranger, but if it hadn't been for them, I would have had no support at all.

Day to day, I was leading a double life. I was one person with Larry and another with everyone but the few medical professionals and counselors who knew about the diagnosis. I put on a false face for my sons, my family, and my friends, making believe that everything was perfect. I couldn't cover my ass fast enough. I was always trying to stay one step ahead so no one could figure out what was really going on. The diagnosis was like a bomb that could detonate at any moment, and I felt it was my job to keep it from exploding.

It was a gargantuan task, and I worried about that impending explosion daily. For a long time, I went to sleep in fear and woke up in fear. And in between, the lies filled me with shame.

I occupied myself with learning everything I could about HIV/AIDS, how to eat right, and how to stay healthy. I learned how to cope with despair in a powerless situation. I became the decision-maker. I was 32 years old, but felt like 100.

It didn't take long for panic attacks to set in. I'd start hyperventilating out of nowhere. And I fought off depression as I kept striving to get rid of Larry's awful virus through sheer will.

One of the things I hated most was having to factor HIV into nearly every decision I made. I couldn't make plans too far into the future because I knew Larry might not still be with us. A shadow was cast over even the fun experiences in our lives. When we went to the kids' school concerts, I wondered how many more Larry would witness. More than once, he said, "I hope I can make it to see Brian graduate from kindergarten."

I was braced for the day when the boys would watch their father waste away and I wouldn't be able to keep the secret from our friends and family anymore. But I had no idea when that day would come. I went from worrying that Larry would come home high to worrying that he would become symptomatic. Essentially, I had traded one obsession for another.

I looked at other parents and envied their lives. I knew no one else was thinking, *This could be the last time we do this together as a family.* The circumstances certainly taught me to cherish every moment, but the fear made it impossible for me to truly enjoy it. The chaos simply wouldn't let up.

Of course, resentment welled up inside me too. I know that's human, but I hated myself for feeling it. I took on most of the responsibility for our situation. I was the one who had had kids with Larry. I was the one who hadn't trusted my instincts and left him years before when I should have.

A part of me wanted to scream at my husband, "What the hell have you done to us?" But I couldn't say such a thing out loud. The man was facing death and the reality of not seeing his young sons grow up. My anger was present, but I didn't feel I had the right to feel it. It was simply easier to blame myself.

So Larry and I kept up our pretense, even when we were alone. Our everyday conversations included the topics most married couples talk about—our kids, playdates, work schedules, and the details of fixing the house. We didn't sit down and have a courageous conversation, like "Honey, I'm so scared about what's going to happen to us when you die." I tried to say this a few times, but I just couldn't make myself say it. I don't think either of us could have borne such a discussion.

My journal became my true confidant during this time. There, I could write down all of my fears and worries without judgment, even though it wasn't as comforting as a trusted friend would have been. I assumed I had very little time to figure out how we were going to make it through, and writing it out in my journal helped me to strategize about how we'd survive once Larry was gone.

I loved our home and our neighborhood. I wanted to be able to keep them for our kids to give them some sense of stability, so I worked hard to leave no stone unturned.

One evening, I saw an ad on late-night TV for life insurance that purportedly didn't require a medical exam. Of course, once you contacted them, they told you that they still expected you to get the exam. So I called and told them we didn't have time for it, to which they said, "Okay, but in that case, you can only buy a policy worth $10,000."

At that time, $10,000 might as well have been $100,000! I found two more companies like that one and got policies that would each pay out $10,000, for a total of $30,000. That gave me some peace of mind, knowing that I would be able to at least pay for a funeral and pay off some bills.

It was a source of embarrassment with my friends, though. They talked about the life insurance policies for $100,000 or more that they'd bought. When they asked me about mine, I lied: "Yes, I bought one of those $100,000 policies." I played the game so no one would know, but inside, I felt like a loser and an outcast.

Health insurance was another serious concern. We had my COBRA coverage from my previous job, but when it ran out, we might not be able to get Larry covered by another policy. I needed to get back to work soon, assuming my entire family would be covered by the company policy without the need for exams.

I also knew I'd soon be the sole supporter of my boys, so I decided to look into returning to FIT to finally finish my degree. I only needed a few more credits.

We couldn't really afford the tuition, but my credits were set to expire in less than six months. We agreed that I would register, and we'd put the tuition on a credit card.

Somehow we'd manage to pay for the gas to Manhattan and the parking.

No one else in our lives could figure out why it was so important to me to go back to school when I had two little kids and a husband whose business was doing reasonably well. I pursued my career with a newfound but quiet urgency, and people in our lives saw me as driven without knowing why.

As we went about our day-to-day lives, one day led to the next, and a year went by as Larry showed no symptoms and continued to be able to work. Then, another year went by . . . and another . . . and another . . . and another. While so many AIDS patients died within months or a year of their diagnosis, Larry just didn't get sick. I even began to entertain the thought that the doctors could be wrong. Maybe he wouldn't die after all. Larry had still never advanced from HIV to AIDS, and he didn't have the lesions and other symptoms that most AIDS patients developed.

The stigma about the disease hadn't eased, though. Those with AIDS were still treated as pariahs, and people remained afraid to even be within breathing distance of someone with the disease. That truth was brought home to us one night when Larry and I watched the movie *Philadelphia*, in which Tom Hanks's character faces that stigma while he dies of AIDS.

Larry started to cry as we watched. "That will never be me," he said. "I'll never waste away like that. I'll kill myself first." I can still feel darkness and death coursing through me whenever I hear Bruce Springsteen's song "Streets of Philadelphia," which he wrote for the film.

Larry saw a number of doctors during the first few years after the diagnosis, but it took five years to find the right one. Dr. Lewis R. Marton was an infectious disease specialist and a godsend. He was not only caring, but also the first doctor in the area to specialize in HIV/AIDS. He had lost his own brother to AIDS, so he had dedicated himself to studying it. He was on the cutting edge of research and treatment. It was a relief that Larry would finally get the best care protocols.

Dr. Marton saw Larry monthly, spending more than four hours with him at each visit and monitoring him carefully. "I'm hesitant to give Larry the usual medications," he told us. "Better meds with fewer side effects are down the road, and if we can just hold out until then, it will be better. Plus, if you get treatment, you might not be eligible for clinical trials. I want Larry to have the chance to be on the most effective medications for HIV. So I'm going to monitor his T-cell count religiously to make sure it's still safe not to medicate him."

A person's T-cell level is an indicator of their immune system's health. Since HIV destroys the immune system, T-cell counts tell doctors how much a patient's health has deteriorated. When an HIV-positive patient's count falls below 200, that person is considered to have AIDS.

Even though Larry's T-cell count continued to drop, it never fell below 250, and he remained without symptoms. No one could tell that his immune system was weakening. He was truly a special case. While he did lose some weight, people were so accustomed to his lankiness that they didn't seem to notice.

Dr. Marton also agreed with our pediatrician about our sons. He felt as long as they didn't show any symptoms, we were safe in not testing them. Meanwhile, Dr. Marton wanted me to participate in a study of people who had been exposed to HIV but hadn't contracted it. In their efforts to find a cure, they were trying to learn if some of us had antibodies that protected us from the virus.

It turned out that I did indeed have an antibody that kept me from getting the disease. That was a huge relief, and it also helped me feel more secure about the safety of the boys.

Finding Dr. Marton helped us to feel a bit more secure, even though we knew it was still a matter of time before Larry got sick. As Larry continued to build his business, he also became obsessed with finishing our own home's renovations before he died. He knew he couldn't leave us much, but this was perhaps a legacy he could provide before it was too late. It was the ultimate act of love on his part, because he knew a real home was what I'd always wanted. I'm sure it was also his way of ensuring that we'd remember him fondly after he was gone.

Still, he went overboard, in my opinion, and it was sometimes alarming how much he wanted to do: Rip the roof off the house. Add more rooms. But there was a limit as to how much time and money he could devote to the house while also trying to build a business and bring in income for us.

I believe Larry was in deep denial about his HIV, perhaps because he was still asymptomatic and felt so confident about Dr. Marton. As a result, he kept expanding the renovations. This meant that the cost also expanded, but he didn't want to think about how we were going to pay for it all.

It just caused me more worry and stress on top of my own worry and stress over Larry's condition. What would happen if he died tomorrow and I was left with this half-finished house? I wouldn't be able to afford to complete it, nor would I be able to sell it unfinished.

Still, I didn't have the heart to say, "Larry, we can't afford all these improvements. What happens if you don't manage to finish?" I knew working on the house was his therapy. It gave him so much happiness, and I knew how much it meant to him to do it for us. He never expressed his feelings to me, but I was aware of the depth of guilt and regret he held inside. And I, once again, hid my worries from him, as well.

As a result of the cost of the renovations, our mortgage, and other expenses, we always seemed to be in catch-up mode financially. Almost every extra dime we had was spent on improving the house. I was continually trying to pay off our credit cards because I knew I wouldn't have much life insurance to help me get out of debt when Larry was gone.

When Brian was about four years old and Little Larry was about nine, my good friend Debbie came up to me while I was on the beach during a two-day vacation with the kids at the Jersey shore. "I'm giving you the keys to my house," she said with a smile on her face.

"Why?"

"Because you're going to need a place to live."

"What do you mean? Why?"

"You'll see" was her only answer.

When I had made my way back to our house, the neighbors started coming outside to see my reaction. We were quite friendly with our neighbors, even if our secret meant our relationships with them were mostly superficial.

When I got close enough to see our house, I stopped in my tracks. It was almost completely leveled. Larry had torn down so much of it that it was no longer livable. Three walls remained, but there was no roof. Plus, there were wires running from the electrical box out to the telephone pole.

Standing in front was my husband with a big smile on his face.

"Oh, my God, what did you do?" I asked him, aghast.

Brian was devastated. "What happened to my house? Where's my stuff, Mommy?" he asked me.

"I rented a big tractor trailer for our stuff," Larry said. "I've already had all of it loaded."

Our neighbors were so thrilled for us. "Isn't this great?" they said.

No, this isn't great! I thought. *How will we pay for this? What if he can't finish it? What will I do then? We won't even have a place to live!*

We never moved in with Debbie. Instead, Larry and his workers put a huge blue tarp over the house and placed our mattresses inside. We slept inside the house under the tarp. It was summer, and we were lucky it didn't rain much that year. But we laughed when we woke up with dew on our faces.

For me, though, the realization came quickly that these precious moments would be the memories we'd call upon after Larry was gone. But within about a month, the house had a frame and roof again. There was still plenty of work to be done, but we could live there without the tarp.

Everyone thought Larry was such a great guy for doing this work on the house for his family, and no one could understand why I wasn't ecstatic. But they didn't know that if he didn't manage to finish, he wasn't going to be the one left to pick up the pieces.

Besides being a killjoy, I also developed a reputation as a nag among my family and friends, even my kids. I hated it. Just as I had always been after him about his addiction recovery, I felt I had to be watchful of his health after the diagnosis. I knew Larry needed to keep his T-cell count as high as possible, so I constantly reminded him to take better care of himself. He would go through phases when he'd be vigilant about taking his vitamins and nutritional supplements. Then he'd become lax and I'd have to remind him again.

A few years after his diagnosis, I grew weary and felt trapped in my role as gatekeeper. Certainly, I didn't want to lose my husband, but it was exhausting being the only responsible adult in the family.

We began to spend Sunday afternoons at my parents' house on a regular basis, but those visits were tainted by my nagging. Both my mom and dad adored Larry and the kids. Their relationships were harmonious with one another, and my relationship with them had improved immensely. So the visits were mostly pleasant.

But then I'd start to worry about all the time we spent there rather than working on the house. I'd say, "Larry, we really have to get back home so you can finish that trim work," or "We really need to get going so you can figure out how to complete the kitchen."

"Come on, Kathe," my dad would say. "Leave the guy alone. He works like a dog!"

I'd also bug Larry to go easy on the beer and cigarettes, because I knew his drinking and smoking would suppress his immune system. Again, my father would intervene. "Let him relax a little while longer and enjoy a drink and a smoke! Why are you always on his case?"

My dad loved me dearly, and even though he didn't know our secret, the two of us were now very close. He was just trying to get me to understand the guys' point of view.

But not being able to explain to anyone why I kept hassling my husband made me feel like an outsider in my own life. My parents and our friends thought I was a control freak and, frankly, a bitch at times. I was the only one who knew my husband was fighting for every

T cell he could get. I knew how vulnerable he was to developing cancer. Yet there he was, smoking cancer-causing cigarettes. I resented Larry for this negative role I felt I was forced to play. It was yet another burden of keeping such a huge secret.

Larry knew exactly why I was so exhausted and frightened. He knew why I was needling him about his health. But he didn't make any effort to make it easier for me. When he hung out with my family and others, it was his chance to be in denial. He knew I wouldn't bitch about his behavior quite as much in front of other people, so he took advantage of every moment.

I wanted to scream, "Everybody cares about Larry, but nobody cares about me! What about *my* pressure, *my* job, and all the responsibilities I have with the kids? I'm trying to keep my husband alive as long as possible! I'm not sitting around smoking cigarettes and drinking beer! Where's *my* escape?" The truth was that I simply didn't have one—not from the reality that my husband was going to die a young man and not from the fact that I couldn't tell my friends or family what I was going through.

While I was feeling like an outsider with our family, I was also feeling like an outsider at work. I'd finished my degree at FIT and been recruited for an exciting position as the regional manager for a new watch company, where I was responsible for a substantial amount of company sales. I was finally building a career.

The job was flexible, and I could make it home in time to give the kids dinner and attend their school games and events. But I was also required to travel quite a bit, which was a high price to pay. This meant I sometimes had to leave the kids with Larry, a man who drank a full six-pack most nights and would drive them around in his pickup truck with a beer in the cup holder. He'd gone from being a functioning drug addict to being a functioning alcoholic with HIV.

Little Larry was old enough at this point to notice and was mortified by his father's behavior. "You're not supposed to drink and drive, Dad." Slowly my eldest son was being robbed of his innocence, which wrenched my heart. He began to take on my role as his father's watchdog when I wasn't around, even though neither of the kids knew about their father's illness or that he might backslide and start using drugs again.

And I was sure Larry wanted to use. After all, he had a death sentence hanging over his head. I was even scared he might try to kill himself with drugs.

When I was out of town, I'd call in the evening to check on Larry and the boys, and it was Little Larry who would fill me in. "I'm doing my homework, and Brian and Daddy are watching TV."

"Did Daddy heat up the dinner I left for you?" I'd ask.

"Yeah, he did. Now they're eating chocolate doughnuts, and Daddy's drinking beer." Since Larry needed to keep his weight up, he could eat anything he wanted, but that didn't mean a little boy should eat chocolate doughnuts and snacks every evening.

Every time I traveled, I wrote a specific schedule and to-do list for Larry to follow while I was gone, but the routine usually broke down after the first couple of nights I was away. I called the house "the bachelor pad" when they were left to fend for themselves.

From Larry's viewpoint, he wasn't doing anything but relaxing with the kids and having a beer or two. It was bonding time for the three of them, and I felt torn. I knew they were making precious memories, but I couldn't help but worry.

Unfortunately, Little Larry was tasked with trying to maintain some of my rules and schedule. "Dad, it's ten o'clock, and Brian should be in bed by now," he'd point out to his father. I hated giving my son so much responsibility at such a young age, but we needed the health insurance and the income my job provided. And I needed to maintain my career so I'd be able to care for the boys when their dad was gone.

Every time I had to leave town, I worried that Larry would be late to pick the kids up at day care or the after-school program, fall asleep with a cigarette burning, or—my worst nightmare—get high. Would his demons come out to play again? I did the best I could to cope, reassuring myself that the nightmare would be over soon and I could then begin to piece my life back together.

I didn't feel like I could ask anyone to help Larry watch the kids, either. How would I have explained that? They wouldn't have understood why they were needed, and I couldn't bear making up more stories and excuses. The lies were weighing on me more and more, as if they were piling up on my body, becoming heavier and heavier.

To say I felt trapped in my circumstances is an understatement. I was in survival mode, operating on raw, gut instinct as I tried to keep the family together.

Ironically, despite all of this madness at home, my bosses and co-workers thought of me as a rock star. I continued to be promoted. Yet I didn't feel that I deserved the accolades I received. Who was I to be celebrated like that? I was a woman with a junkie husband dying of HIV.

My co-workers were experienced and well-educated people. As they swapped stories about their college years, I'd think, *I was virtually homeless at that time in my life.* Our spouses were invited to join us at extravagant sales meetings on tropical islands, but I'd arrive alone, making up excuses for why my husband couldn't join me. "My husband is so wonderful," I told them. "He doesn't mind taking care of the kids while I work."

Work conversations would include my co-workers' future plans: "We're going to have another kid," or "We're looking at larger houses." They'd ask me about my kids and often wanted to connect outside of work and become friends. But I kept my homelife private, never mixing the two.

It looked to me like everybody had a normal life *but* me. It took me right back to my childhood. I feared exposure and couldn't take any chances with my career or income. I felt that I had gained entry through one of those coveted doors on my childhood street, and I wouldn't do anything to risk my place inside. That meant the weight of the lies just kept piling on.

Would my colleagues have shunned me if they'd known the reality of my life? Would they have reacted as I feared? Would I still have advanced in my career as I did? I have no way of knowing. All I knew was that most people still saw HIV and AIDS as a modern plague, and I didn't feel I could take a chance on telling them, not when I knew I'd soon have to take care of the boys alone.

One day, about seven years after Larry's diagnosis, we ran into a friend unexpectedly. "Oh, my God, you look like you have AIDS," she said to Larry. She wasn't serious, but Larry's health was finally beginning to fail. People could see that he'd grown way too thin and pale. They just didn't know why. I was the only one who saw him struggle through his aches and pains to get out of bed every morning. Clearly, we wouldn't be able to hide the truth much longer.

Dr. Marton was finally forced to put Larry on about 20 different medications. After that, the combination of the illness and the side effects caused his hair to thin and his eyesight to diminish. As his immune system failed, he repeatedly came down with colds and coughs that everyone assumed he was catching from the kids. He tried his best to hide his symptoms, putting on a brave face even at home so the boys wouldn't worry. But he couldn't hide any of it from me.

Even though the boys were still young, it was also becoming more difficult to keep the secret from them. Little Larry was getting old enough to question why there were so many bottles of pills in the breadbox. I'd always try to distract him with made-up reasons like "Oh, Dad just got a little infection." But my son wasn't easy to fool. He was smart, and his dad's thinning hair and weight loss were harder to explain.

Before long, Larry couldn't drink beer anymore without getting sick, and as his sight deteriorated, I worried that he'd have to stop driving and working. Cigarettes were his last remaining vice.

He was officially ill, and the end was sneaking up on us. Somehow, though, he was able to keep going, climbing ladders and working on roofs. I think he continued out of sheer will, determined to go until he dropped, probably motivated by both guilt and love.

While I admired my husband for getting up and working every day when he felt so weak, I was disturbed by his refusal to talk to me about how he was feeling physically and emotionally. There was no discussion, so I didn't even have Larry to talk to about it all. As a result, I felt even more alone. It was just me and my secrets.

Maybe because I knew Larry's symptoms meant his diagnosis would probably come out before long, the burden of hiding and always covering my tracks was becoming unbearable. It was rare for someone with an HIV diagnosis to live as long as Larry did, and I'd never expected to have to protect him for so long. It kept our lives on hold in every way. I was happy my husband was still alive; the last thing I wanted was to lose him. But I was exhausted from making up stories about why he wasn't feeling well. "Oh, he's got the flu again." "He drank too much last night." "He ate something that didn't agree with him."

Lying went against every moral principle I held dear. With my integrity long gone out the window, I started to feel like my whole life was an illusion. I even began to lose my grip on what was real and what wasn't. I didn't have HIV, but secrecy was its own kind of virus living inside me.

CHAPTER 7

THE FINAL BLOW

In 1995, I just couldn't bear keeping Larry's diagnosis from everyone any longer. It was a pressure cooker inside of me.

The first person I told was someone outside of the family. I had met my friend Debbie when Little Larry and her oldest son were in kindergarten together. We spent hours in the park talking while the boys played and soon became best friends. Not long after, her husband, Vince, became Larry's best friend as well. We even spent weekends together. But our best friends still didn't know about Larry's illness.

One day, I was sitting at Debbie's kitchen table, complaining about Larry. She protested, "But Larry's doing so great!"

I knew if I told her the truth, it might put our friendship in jeopardy. Maybe she wouldn't want to spend time with me anymore. But I couldn't stand pretending with her for one more second. I trusted and loved Debbie. If I could tell anyone outside of the family, it would be her. So that day in her kitchen, I started crying.

"What's wrong?" Debbie asked.

"I have to tell you something."

"What is it?" She could tell it was serious, but I'm sure what ran through her head in that moment was that Larry was having an affair or an alcohol problem, or that we were facing bankruptcy. The last thing you'd expect to hear from a heterosexual couple at that time was that someone had HIV.

"I know you think Larry's doing great, but he isn't. He's very sick."

Debbie looked at me with alarm and concern.

"He's had HIV for years, and he's going to die. He got it when he was shooting drugs years ago."

"What? No! Kathe, no! It can't be!"

I couldn't believe I'd actually said it out loud. I felt immense relief, as if I'd been sprung from a jail cell after years of incarceration, but I also felt tremendous guilt. I immediately wanted to take back every word. I'd betrayed my beloved. Who the hell was I to have done that?

Thankfully, Debbie just listened as years of emotions came flooding out of me. I suddenly had license to express my worries, fears, and even my anger. I begged her to understand that my frustration and hurt didn't negate my love for Larry.

In a moment that neither one of us will ever forget, she said, "Let it out; let it go," as she held me with such tenderness.

I pleaded with her not to tell her husband, who was a cop, and I asked her not to ever let on to Larry that she knew. It was so important that he not feel like a freak around his friends. Of course, it was the same kind of secrecy that he'd perpetuated as a drug addict. Now Debbie was infected with the secret too.

I'd been living and hiding within Larry's story for so many years. When I told Debbie, it was the first moment I had allowed myself to step out of his story, if only for a short time. I broke my husband's confidence, but I told Debbie for my own sanity. I did it for me. I didn't know it at the time, but it was an act of self-preservation.

Still, for weeks after I told her, I couldn't shake the fear that she'd decide to stop being my friend. I worried that she'd tell Vince and they'd say, "We don't want Larry in our house," or "We don't want our kids around you." But none of that ever happened. Debbie truly loved me unconditionally, and that was a kind of love I'd never experienced in my life.

In so much of my life, there had been triangle configurations. I'd ended up in the middle between my mother and father, my mother and brother, my father and brother, my mother and grandmother, or my father and my husband. With Debbie, there was no triangle. She saw me and loved me, and she also loved my husband and children. There was no conflict or opposition. It was just a beautiful, unbroken circle of love.

When Debbie learned that no one else knew, not even my parents, she was blown away. She gave me the support, encouragement, and courage I needed to be able to tell them next.

I started with my mother. But I didn't tell her without a great deal of agonizing. I knew all too well that she might react as I feared, giving me that "You've made your bed, so go lie in it" line again.

But she didn't react that way at all. "Oh, my God, not Larry! You poor kids!" she said. "How have you lived with this for so long? Why didn't you tell us?"

When we told my dad, he was equally upset that I hadn't told them sooner. They were devastated to think we'd all be losing Larry before long. They were both instantly supportive, which was such a gift for me. I truly needed help, because after so many years of carrying it all on my own shoulders, I was close to crumbling. They became more attentive, coming by to check in on us more often and babysitting the boys. Mostly, though, they just listened as I talked about my fears and pain. It was such a relief to talk about my feelings after keeping them bottled up for so long.

Next, I asked Larry about telling his mother. "Larry, it isn't fair to your mother to keep it from her any longer. What are you going to do, just have her show up all of a sudden when you're on your deathbed? She'll be blind-sided. And I'm not going to be put in the position of having to tell her after you're gone and trying to explain why you wanted to keep it from her. As a mom, I think it's a selfish thing to do to her. If my kids did that to me, I'd be so hurt and wouldn't want my memory of them to be tainted by that."

Finally, he agreed to tell her, but I knew it would be one of the hardest things he'd ever done. He loved his mother and hated the thought of hurting her. Before he had a chance, though, something happened.

Even though Larry's T-cell count was still high enough that he hadn't developed AIDS, Dr. Marton discovered that Larry was riddled with lymphoma, a type of cancer that attacks the lymph nodes. "I never expected it could spread so quickly," he told us. A tumor in Larry's spleen had already been found, but because it was benign, Dr. Marton had decided to leave it alone until it was absolutely necessary to deal with it.

Meanwhile, he sent us to Memorial Sloan Kettering Cancer Center, where Larry saw a top oncologist. "There's nothing we can do," the doctor told us. "The cancer has already spread so much that lymph node surgery just isn't a viable option, and Larry's body is much too weak for chemotherapy or radiation."

We'd known this day would come, but that didn't make it any less devastating. Reality was staring us right in the face. Larry began to cry. He could no longer deny that he was going to die. There was no turning back, no more hope, no more miracles. "Let's just make it through Christmas," we said to each other.

Within a few weeks of receiving the lymphoma diagnosis, Larry's spleen tumor caused him so much pain that we had to rush him to the emergency room. It was Halloween of 1995, nearly eight years since his diagnosis, and miraculously, it became the first time he was hospitalized in all that time.

Halloween was always a big event at our house. The boys were dressed up in their costumes, ready for trick-or-treating, when we took their dad to the hospital. Little Larry, who was 11 years old, was afraid to go to the hospital. It was too frightening for him, so I didn't push him. Instead, he stayed home and went trick-or-treating with Debbie and her children.

Six-year-old Brian, on the other hand, wanted to see his dad. Still in his costume, he crawled right into the hospital bed.

That's when I called Larry's mother and stepfather in Florida. I told them only that he had a tumor in his spleen, and I asked them to fly to New Jersey. When they arrived at the hospital, I said, "Larry needs to speak to his mother."

His stepfather didn't understand. "What do you mean? I flew all the way here from Florida, and I can't see him?"

"Look, he just needs a little time with his mother first, okay?" Larry then told her the truth about his HIV status. She was overcome, of course, but she handled it well, perhaps better than I would have in her shoes.

Neither she nor Larry's stepfather were angry that he'd kept it from them for so long. With three children who had become drug addicts, Larry's mom had often gone into denial to cope, which I thoroughly understood.

After a few days, Larry was discharged from the hospital, and Dr. Marton suggested that we schedule surgery to remove the spleen tumor soon.

Larry's weight loss became even more pronounced following his hospital stay. He began to look utterly emaciated. We'd go to the boys' ball games and people would tease him—"Hey, there, Larry, you're getting awful skinny. Are you okay, man?" He hated how he looked and tried to cover it up by wearing his winter coat. He had to admit to himself that he was beginning to look like Tom Hanks's character in *Philadelphia* after all.

Even though he still didn't officially have AIDS or any lesions on his body, it became harder and harder to pretend, even with strangers, that Larry was a healthy person.

As Christmas approached, my mother convinced us that we should go away for the weekend while she watched the kids for us. We went to New Hope, Pennsylvania, and stayed at a bed-and-breakfast. We were so emotionally drained by this time that there was little for us to talk about. Without the boys around as a distraction, we were confronted with one another and the reality that this would be our last Christmas together. As much as we wanted to make the time together count, the energy between us was tense.

We walked around the village and bought Christmas ornaments for the boys. But Larry was understandably despondent, and I felt rejected. By the time we got back to our room, years of pent-up anger and fear poured out of me. I knew the end was coming, and I wanted him to know that I was petrified to be without him. I wanted him to protect me from the pain just once before he died.

"Look what you did to our lives!" I blurted out. "I'm not even forty, and I've been through hell and back! And now, what? What's going to happen to me and the boys?"

"I know," he said softly. "I'm so sorry."

As I continued my rant, Larry shut down. But I couldn't stop. I was overcome with grief, and I wanted him to admit how much he'd impacted my life and his sons' lives.

But he didn't say a word. He just sat there and took it.

When I was spent, I felt shocked and ashamed of myself. *How could I be so selfish?* I thought. *Did I really have to make him feel all of this?*

I started to sob. "I never should have said all of those horrible things. I'm so sorry."

"I never realized that I hurt you so bad," he said.

In that moment, I became aware of the full extent of Larry's denial. How could he not have known how deeply I was hurting? But I also became aware of just how much armor I'd been wearing and how dangerous it was to hide your emotions to such a degree. If I'd known how to give my feelings a healthy outlet, I probably wouldn't have had such an outburst.

The next morning, I realized that we were both finally surrendering to reality and saying good-bye to each other. As painful as it was, I believe it was necessary for us.

With the pent-up anger released, we could be together in a different way as our family celebrated Christmas. We knew it would be our last together as a family, so, bittersweet as it was, we were determined to make it the best Christmas our children had ever had. He bought me a beautiful ring as his final gift to me, and we got the boys the best gifts we could think of.

Early in 1996, we took the boys to a therapist named Pat to help us begin the process of telling them. Larry and I had started seeing her for couples therapy a few months earlier, but we hadn't had time to make much progress. She had only seen the boys three or four times when I planned a trip to Florida to see if we could move there.

The medications that Larry had to take made him so sensitive to cold that New Jersey winters were becoming intolerable. Since Florida was part of my sales territory, I had hatched a plan that maybe I could get transferred there, where the warm weather would be easier on Larry. We'd be close to his parents, who could help out when his illness became more than I could handle.

"I'm worried about you working so hard. I think you're going to have to stop soon," I told him. "I've been carrying it all for a long time, but it's going to become more than I can do without help. My parents aren't going to be able to do it, but maybe your mom would."

So on this trip, I thought I would talk to my boss in Florida about relocating and pay Larry's parents a visit to ask for help.

As always on the night before I traveled, we went over the schedule and long to-do list that I was leaving for Larry and the boys. As we were driving home from a trade show at the Javits Center, I asked him about his day to gauge whether he was prepared, and that's when my cross-examination began.

"What did you do today? Did you take your medicine? Did you talk to the doctor?"

He just wanted me to leave him alone. In the back of my mind, I was aware that the kids were in the back seat, probably listening to everything we said and wondering why their dad needed a doctor, but I just couldn't let it go. I fired questions at him not to bug him, but to reassure myself that he'd take proper care of the boys, as well as himself. Rather than leaving them alone with him, I'd have preferred to have my parents or Debbie come over to help, but I knew my husband well enough to know that he would send them home, insisting that he could handle it.

As a result of my needling, there was a lot of tension in the air when Larry and I went to bed. The next morning, there was little conversation between us before I left for the airport.

Once I arrived in Florida, I spent the day working and met his parents for dinner. "I think Larry's getting sick," I blurted out over the entrées. They had only known about his HIV status for about three months, and we still hadn't told them about the lymphoma. As far as they knew, he just had a benign tumor in his spleen.

When I saw the look of panic in his mother's eyes, I backtracked a bit. I spent the rest of the meal trying to walk a fine line between asking for their help and reassuring them that everything would be okay (even though I was really the one who needed reassuring).

I was spending the night at their house, and I called home to check in before going to bed. Little Larry answered the phone.

"How are things going, sweetheart?" I asked.

"Something's wrong with Daddy," he replied. I could tell by his voice that he was terrified.

"What do you mean? What's wrong?" I asked, trying to keep my voice upbeat so my son wouldn't become even more worried.

"It's like he keeps falling asleep and then waking up, and then falling asleep again."

I started to panic, thinking, *Drugs? Alcohol? Has Larry relapsed?* Dr. Marton had gotten Larry into some clinical trials over the years that had required travel into

Manhattan for blood work. I'd always worried that he'd drive up to Harlem and get high. Would he have gotten high while alone with the kids?

I tried to get more information out of my son without alarming him, but he started to cry. I didn't want to press him and traumatize him further.

"Call Aunt Kris and ask her to come over right away. Then tell her to call me, okay?"

My sister lived just one town over, and by this time, she knew about Larry's diagnosis. She was two months pregnant, so I hated to bother her. But I couldn't leave the kids to handle the situation on their own.

Before Kris arrived, Larry passed out and fell on the floor. Both of my little boys hunched over their father. They were hysterical, trying anything they could think of to awaken their dad. "Do this!" Brian said. "Try this!" Then, just moments before Kris got there, Larry came out of it. Just like that.

She called me and said, "He's absolutely fine," and handed Larry the phone.

"I don't know what happened, but I'm just going to go to bed." He sounded groggy, but mostly like himself.

"Do you think you should go to the hospital?"

"No, I just want to get a good night's sleep."

"Okay, but call Dr. Marton in the morning. I'll be home soon."

I suppose I should have tried to make him go to the hospital, but I knew I wouldn't win that argument. Thank God that Kris and her husband, David, were willing to stay the night to make sure everything was all right. Kris calmed Brian and Larry down, made sure their homework was done, and got them safely into bed.

The next morning, Kris helped the boys get ready for school. But when they checked on Larry, he was unresponsive. It was Valentine's Day—February 14, 1996.

At about 6:30 A.M., David called me in Florida.

"Kathe, I'm so sorry to have to tell you this, but Larry's dead," he said. As soon as I heard the words, I fell to the floor and started screaming unlike any screaming I'd ever uttered before. The sound woke up Larry's parents, who came running.

"No! No! No!" I shouted repeatedly.

How could he die without me there? I thought. *I never should have left. I knew better. I could feel it.*

Kris had called 911, and when the police arrived, they wanted to talk to me on the phone. "Was he sick? Was something wrong with him? Did you know this was coming?" I could feel the anxiety welling up inside me. They needed to know, especially those who would be handling Larry's body.

"I have to tell you something, but you can't tell anyone. Promise me!" The officer didn't respond, so I repeated it. "Promise me!" I pleaded with him.

"Okay," he said.

I took a deep breath and let it out. "He's HIV-positive." I could only hope to God that they would keep our secret.

After I got off the phone, I focused on getting home as fast as possible. I booked the first flight back, which turned out to be the last one available before a big winter storm grounded all planes headed for the Northeast.

As I sat wedged into my seat on the plane, my mind was spinning in all directions. My worst nightmare had just happened. It had actually happened. And my last moments with Larry had been tense. I was grateful that we'd had such a wonderful Christmas after our emotional time in New Hope. I was comforted by the knowledge that Larry did know how much I loved him.

But I chastised myself. *You never should have left. You knew he wasn't himself. You didn't trust your instincts.*

Then I fought with myself further. *But I had to go. I had to try to get us set up in Florida, where we'd have help. Oh, God. Why'd it have to happen while I was away? My poor little boys. Why now?*

I tried to reckon with the truth. *Larry's gone. I can't believe he's actually gone.* No matter how much you know a death is coming, you can never be prepared for it.

And then I worried about what was going to happen next. Would the police keep our secret? How was I going to plan a service? I'd heard funeral homes didn't want to take people with HIV, so I thought that maybe I shouldn't tell them. No, no, I would have to tell them, I knew.

But what would I tell our friends, Larry's clients, everyone? They were going to ask questions. They'd want to know why. What was I going to say? If people knew, would they shun us? Would they be afraid the rest of us were infected and turn away? I felt certain that there would be people in our lives who would do exactly that. I couldn't bear the thought of my sons enduring such judgment at the same time that they were dealing with the loss of their father.

Worst of all, how was I going to tell them about their dad? I had to get to my boys. I had to hold them. They needed me, and I needed them. How would I go about telling them something so horrible? And how would I answer when they asked, "Why did Daddy die?" Little Larry was only 12, and Brian was just 7.

I'd just lost the love of my life, but there was no time to process my grief or worry about myself. And through it all, I still had this secret to protect from all but a handful of people.

It was the longest plane ride of my life.

I don't even recall how I got home from the airport. When I arrived, the kids were still at school, but the house was filled with people from the neighborhood, some of whom I didn't know very well at all. They had lovingly brought food and were sitting in the living room and at the kitchen table. As I suspected, they wanted to know how Larry had died. All I wanted to do was collapse, not answer questions.

While I knew everyone had the best intentions, their presence felt like such an intrusion. I was entering my home, where my husband had died just hours before. Within a very short time, I would have to tell my kids that their father was dead. The last thing I wanted to see were unfamiliar faces at my kitchen table. The only people I wanted around were family members and my absolute best friends.

I wanted to say, "Get the hell out of my house!" But I couldn't say such a thing to well-meaning people. I felt I just had to swallow and endure my feelings.

Debbie looked at me and could see from my expression how I felt. She did what she could to shield me from questions and encouraged people to go.

Little Larry arrived home from school less than an hour after I got home. I was still far from prepared to tell the boys. Of course, the first thing my eldest son wanted to know was if his dad was okay. I think on some level, he already knew. We went upstairs to my bedroom, and I told him that his father was gone. He dissolved into tears, and I held him tight as we cried together.

Since Little Larry had ended up parenting his dad more than the other way around, their relationship had been complicated. The two of them had butted heads when my son chided his father for drinking too much or not putting Brian to bed early enough. Luckily, they had drawn closer as they discovered their mutual affection for music. That was a blessing amidst the pandemonium of our household, and I'm grateful Little Larry found a special way to connect with his dad.

Brian's relationship with his father was different. He simply loved his father. When he came home soon after his brother that day, the news of Larry's death overtook him. He grabbed me and wouldn't let go. His body trembled, and he couldn't speak. He cried silently, as if the tears were bleeding from him.

He held on to me like that, not letting go. I could feel a tangible shift in his body as I think the reality of his father's death truly set in. My innocent little boy was gone forever, and he withdrew into himself. The three of us lay in bed, holding on to each other for a long time.

It was heart-wrenching to know that there was little I could do to protect my sons from the worst pain of life. That day, we all lost parts of ourselves and entered into a black hole of grief.

Later, as I tried to sleep, I'm certain Larry's spirit came to me. I woke up in the middle of the night, and the room was ice-cold. There was no doubt in my mind that it was him. Yet I was too petrified to open my eyes and look. What would I do if I actually saw his spirit there?

He never came to me again after that, and I worried that he'd felt rejected because I wouldn't open my eyes that evening. But I couldn't bear saying good-bye.

The next day, after a sleepless night, Larry's doctor's office called with the results of a brain scan they'd conducted on him a few days earlier. "Mrs. Crawford, you need to get your husband to the hospital immediately. We found cancer in his brain. He could die at any moment."

"Well, you're too late. He died at home yesterday morning," I told the nurse matter-of-factly. I was numb by this point.

"Oh, Mrs. Crawford, I'm so sorry."

To keep my sanity and strength during the years after Larry's diagnosis, I had often told myself that life would get easier in some ways after he was gone. It was a coping mechanism, I guess. I knew I would miss him beyond fathoming, but at least there would be no more waiting for the bomb to go off. No more doctor's appointments or medications in the breadbox. No more nagging him to take care of himself. No more stories to tell about why he'd been in the hospital or why we couldn't make plans. I'd thought that some of that heaviness would lift. But I was so wrong. Living without Larry proved to be even harder.

CHAPTER 8

LIVING WITHOUT LARRY

"Your heart is like the bottom of an old shipwreck, encrusted in a protective shell of barnacles. This shell shields you from the pain and suffering you've experienced. It's been your way of coping all of these years," my meditation and spiritual teacher, Ramananda John E. Welshons, told me a few years ago, long after Larry's death.

At first, I resisted this characterization of my heart. But then I realized its truth and could easily visualize my overburdened heart, each barnacle representing my grief and my secrets.

In armoring my heart against the possibility of pain, I had also prevented myself from feeling joy and accepting love from myself or anyone else. That armor of barnacles kept me stuck. I thought back to the many times in my life when I had felt that I was physically dragging the barnacles around with me. At times, that weight had been more than I could carry.

To a large degree, during our last years together, my love for my husband had been strangled by those barnacles around my heart. It had been my way of protecting myself from the full onslaught of losing the love of my life.

But once he was gone, I couldn't hide from that loss anymore. I was painfully aware of how deeply I had loved the man regardless of his faults and what he'd put us through. Losing him hurt so much more than I had ever imagined.

When Larry died, the barnacles didn't go with him. The weight felt even heavier. And I was simply broken.

I had faced so many challenges when he was alive, but suddenly, I had a whole new set of challenges. I was truly on my own, and I still felt that I had to safeguard his secret, both to protect his memory and to protect my sons.

I had been fortunate to find a funeral director who was exceedingly kind about Larry's HIV status. There was a big snowstorm the day of the funeral, and the boys, my dad, and my brother were in the car with me as I drove to the funeral home. On our way, the R.E.M. song "It's the End of the World as We Know It" came on the radio. Little Larry heard it first—"Listen, listen!"

The boys and I had long played a game in which we'd mark certain important moments in our lives. If something unique happened, whether happy or sad, I'd say to them, "This is something to put in your memory bank and lock it in!"

When the R.E.M. song began to play, I said, "Okay, this is one of those things. Put it in your memory bank."

The snow was more of a deterrent to our drive than I had anticipated, so by the time we arrived, we were more than a half hour late. Everyone was waiting for us.

But Brian refused to get out of the car. I understood exactly how he felt; I didn't want to get out of the car, either. He couldn't comprehend the reality of attending his own father's funeral. All the men in my family had been born under the astrological sign of Taurus, but Brian was the most stubborn of the three of them. He was also enormously sensitive, with a tendency to hide his emotions. He had learned well from his parents.

I could tell when I looked in his eyes that he didn't know how to handle that his whole life had changed. How could he, at the tender age of seven?

I didn't want to go inside without Brian, but my dad persuaded me. "You're already so late. You've got to get in there." Reluctantly, I left my youngest son in the car with my brother, who would try to convince Brian to go inside.

When I walked in, I looked around the funeral home's surreal interior. It was very colonial, which felt so wrong for Larry. *He'd absolutely hate this*, I thought. *He must be rolling over in his grave.*

Several people at the funeral were annoyed that we were late, but I felt like saying, "Fuck all of you!" Almost no one there had any idea of what we'd been through. So many people showed up from my sons' elementary school, middle school, and high school. People from work. People from Larry's business. Distant family members. Acquaintances I didn't know well. Larry had been so popular that there had actually been a line to get inside.

They were all there with the best of intentions, but I wasn't prepared for so many of them. I didn't think, *Look at all these people who care about us.* Instead, I thought, *Oh, my God, look at all these people!*

The truth is that the community was stunned that Larry had died. They'd had no idea that he was ill, even though some must have suspected it as he'd started to look less than healthy.

Some of the kids' teachers and coaches were exceptionally nosy and seemed put out by our secrecy. "What on earth happened? You never told us that your son's father was sick!"—as if I'd been obligated to tell them. One of Little Larry's coaches even took my son into another room and had a conversation with him without my permission. I had no idea what he was saying to my little boy. I felt that I'd lost control of everything.

But I had to tell people something, so I just told everyone that Larry had died of cancer. It wasn't a lie, although it was far from the whole story.

In my grief, it was more exhausting than ever to play my usual role. Thankfully, my parents were very protective of me in those moments, doing their best to shield me from the endless prying.

The reality is that the funeral was a beautiful outpouring of love for my husband, but for me that day, in my traumatized state, it seemed like a freak show. I couldn't take in the compassion and love that people were trying to express. Everything had been so personal between Larry and me, and suddenly I felt exposed.

I'm told that I fell into the arms of some people and told them how much it meant to me that they were there, but I have no recollection of this. Even now, my memory of much of that day is a blur.

Debbie's husband, Vince, who loved Larry, was the perfect person to give the eulogy. Since Larry had been such a laid-back guy, he'd sometimes just say "Fuck it!" if he couldn't control, fix, or change a situation. It had become a running joke between Larry and anyone who knew him. At one point during the eulogy, Vince said, "You know what Larry would say . . . ," and everyone in the funeral home held their breath, hoping that Vince wouldn't say something so irreverent out loud. He didn't, but they all knew exactly what he meant, and everyone shared a bittersweet moment of humor.

When Brian finally came inside with my brother, he immediately climbed onto my lap and refused to move. I was just as traumatized as he was, and it was comforting to have him in my arms.

Brian was afraid to look at his father's body in the open casket. He closed his eyes and covered his face so he wouldn't have to see. He'd never been to a funeral or seen a dead body, so I can only imagine how frightening it must have been for him.

When everyone else had exited, including Little Larry, who was with my parents, I persuaded Brian to go up to the casket with me, just the two of us. I took his hand and said, "Let's go say good-bye to Dad. I know you don't want to do this, but this is the last time you'll get to see him. Someday, in your heart, you'll be glad you did." He trusted me, so he walked up with me and bravely looked at his father. I was so proud of the courage he showed in that moment. Little Larry then came back in and joined us. Suddenly, we were three instead of four.

Just a few days after the funeral, I had to contend with more questions about the circumstances of Larry's death. When had he been diagnosed with cancer? Why did it kill him so quickly? At least the cancer story was mostly believable because we'd already told some people about the tumor in his spleen. It explained why he had been in the hospital months before and why he'd been scheduled to go into the hospital for surgery during the week following his death.

Still, people were surprised by how abruptly he'd died. Even Dr. Marton, who knew more about Larry's condition than anyone, was surprised by it.

Soon, however, I discovered that there was more to his death than even I had known.

There had been a dramatic scene at my house the day after Larry died when his sister showed up talking about her husband, Sully. "Larry contacted Sully that night and wanted him to buy some dope," she insisted on telling me. I wanted to lunge and choke her. Luckily, I was surrounded by family, who intervened.

"You get the hell out of here, and don't ever come back," my father shouted at her. While the thought had crossed my mind the night before Larry died, I didn't want to believe it.

Then, a few days after Larry's death, I found a spoon in the kitchen silverware drawer. It had been Little Larry's spoon when he was younger. But now, it had telltale burn marks on it. It was a small, deep spoon—perfect for cooking heroin. And I knew that Larry's sister might have been right. Larry could have gotten high the night before he died.

Rage burned through me. The feeling of betrayal was all-encompassing. *This is how you leave us?* I thought. *How could you do that to your children?*

As angry as I felt, I was also heartbroken that my husband had given up and that the truth was even uglier than I had realized. Anger, grief, love, exhaustion—I felt the gamut and broke down in a crush of tears.

I had to concede that Larry must have felt the gamut too. He'd been dying a painful death. He must have thought, *I'm not going to waste away in a hospice bed with sores all over my body, just waiting to die.* If he'd gotten in touch with his brother-in-law, it meant he'd wanted a sure thing—someone he could count on to get the dope for him. And he'd had to do it when I wasn't home. It was his window of opportunity—the only way out, as he saw it. He was tired, he was dying, and he didn't want to fight anymore. He was done. Oh, God.

Of course, I can't be sure of what was going on in my husband's head; I can only speculate based on what I knew about him. And I'm sure no one knew him better than me.

Besides the secrets, the grief, and the anger, I felt enormous guilt that I hadn't been there when Larry died. How could I ever forgive myself for what my boys had endured? If only we'd been able to arrange for our better life in Florida, as I'd planned. Larry could've stayed warm there and been cared for when I had to work.

When I found the spoon, however, my instincts were once again to be secretive and to protect my husband's memory. I immediately hid it away and kept it to myself. In fact, I hid it away for years. I believe I got rid of it many years later, but to this day, I'm not sure.

So I had yet another secret to keep—Larry's overdose or fatal shot the night before he died.

Since it had been so exhausting to keep up the pretense for so many years, you'd think I would have let Larry's secrets go after his death. After all, he wasn't around anymore for me to protect. But I was still the guardian of his memory and the shield between my sons and the awful truth.

There was something more that kept me holding on to the secrets, however. They were the only connection I had left with my husband. I just couldn't give that up.

Simply put, Larry's secret had become my secret. His story was my story.

Once my sons and I settled back into our lives, we had to find a way to keep living—without Larry. None of us knew how to begin or how to go on, but I suppose that's true for anyone who experiences a shattering loss. Somehow, you have to force yourself to get out of bed every morning and place one foot in front of the other.

I felt I had to put my own grief on a shelf in order to be there for my sons emotionally and physically. Both of them were devastated, but because of the difference in their ages, each experienced it in his own way.

Little Larry once said to me, "Daddy died on Valentine's Day. What happens if I ever fall in love? It'll always be a very sad day." I didn't know what to do but hug him. It was true that his Valentine's Days would always carry that memory.

Then he asked his grandfather, "Who's going to teach me how to shave?" Of course, my dad said he would teach him, but my heart twisted into a knot at the knowledge that my boys would miss such important father-son moments.

Neither of my sons became disruptive at school, but they both hated the attention they got from everyone because their father had died—especially Brian. He went from being the cutest little boy with big eyes, a dynamite smile, and a sandy-blond bowl haircut to a boy who didn't smile anymore.

He felt like an outcast, different from all of his classmates because they had fathers. "I'm not playing sports anymore because I don't have a dad. If you're on a team, you need a dad who goes to the games," he said. He believed his life couldn't be normal anymore.

I was especially concerned because Brian wouldn't talk about how he felt. Little Larry tried to be strong and supportive. I felt I had to do something to help them through it, so I started reading books about how losing a parent affects children. One of the books mentioned art therapy to help kids express grief nonverbally. I found an art therapist for them and also continued to take them to see our therapist, Pat, since they knew her and she'd known Larry.

Once, in the car on the way to art therapy, Little Larry said, "We're really okay, you know."

"Yeah, we are," Brian chimed in.

It was a long drive once a week to get to the art therapist's, and they knew it was stressful for me. But I said, "No, you've got to process this. You need therapy to be healthy. Someday, you're going to thank me for this."

While I can't quantify how much it helped them, I'm certain it did. And in that time following Larry's death, the three of us became a unit. We made a pact with one another that we'd stick together forever. We'd talk about what our lives were going to be like: "Someday you'll both get married, and I'll have grandchildren. Won't that be cool?"

I kept pictures of Larry all over the house. We talked about him a lot, including what it would have been like if he'd lived. The boys imagined that his business would have become more successful, and we would have moved to an affluent town to live in a huge house that Larry built for us.

Like I had when my husband first left me with Little Larry, I made sure we found fun activities to do together. We continued to go to museums, playgrounds, and events whenever we could.

About three weeks after Larry's death, I went back to work. My company had been very understanding about my absence; no one had pressured me to return. But I wanted some semblance of normalcy. Plus, there were financial concerns.

Larry had come close to completing the home renovations, but I had no way to finance what was left unfinished—two bathrooms and a few other areas. Meanwhile, I had credit card bills, medical bills, and some remaining business debts from Larry's company that I had to address. The town we lived in had an inadequate public school system, so I struggled to afford to send the boys to their Catholic school.

Still, going back to work was tough. I was barely holding it together, and finding it difficult to eat or sleep. When the days were finished and the boys had been fed and put to bed, I cried. Whenever I was alone, I was crying. Larry had been the center of my universe for 15 years, and being without him just didn't seem possible.

I was so paralyzed with grief that the only thing that kept me going was my love for my sons. If it hadn't been for them, I probably would have sat on a park bench and watched life pass me by. My mind constantly raced with all sorts of thoughts about what was going to happen to us, what I could have done differently, how screwed up my life was, and on and on.

Time passed, but I couldn't imagine that the grief would ever end. I felt caught in a web. Happiness felt utterly unattainable. In spite of all the times in my life when I'd felt alone, I never felt more alone than after Larry's death.

I was only 39. *How am I going to make it through another 40 years of this life?* I wondered. I was obsessed with the fact that my pain would never subside and that I would live like this the rest of my life. *If I were 70 and lost my husband, I wouldn't have to live that much longer without him.*

Still, I never let anyone see me hurting. So hardly anyone thought to ask, "Hey, Kathe, are you okay?" Of course, I often didn't ask for help, either. Thankfully, my parents did help, and Debbie was always there for me.

What I missed the most was that when Larry knew I was overwhelmed, he would put his arm around me, hold me close, and pat me on the shoulder. "Don't worry, it'll be okay," he'd say. It was something I'd longed for throughout my childhood. When I shared this with my parents, they smiled and hugged me tight. How many people get a second chance at their relationship with their parents? It was certainly one of the blessings in my life in the midst of all the sorrow.

As wonderful as those moments were, they were only a temporary respite from the emotion that threatened to overtake me every day. I had huge mood swings and desperately wanted a sense of peace.

I tried bereavement groups, but there I was, the 40-year-old sitting with 60- and 70-year-olds. No one could relate to me, and I couldn't relate to them. When I shared my story, I had to keep everything so general: "My husband got cancer. He was sick." Feeling that I couldn't tell the truth kept me isolated from everyone in the group.

Since sleep was elusive for a long time, I started to get up at four or five in the morning to take walks. Before long, that evolved into running, even though I had never been an athletic person. Eventually, I was running five miles a day—in the rain, in the sleet, and in the snow. I got special picks for the soles of my sneakers so I wouldn't slip in winter weather. With music playing in my earbuds, my mind stopped racing. It was the only way I found escape, and it was my way of feeling strong and in control of my body. I suppose it also helped me to release endorphins.

Over time, people in the community got to know my routine and waved at me from their cars on their way to work.

At the same time, I continued to advance in my career, gaining credibility in my industry. The new visibility at work meant I had to lead meetings, trainings, and seminars. My kids were my biggest fans, often helping me prepare for my presentations. They'd test me on what I had to learn and assist me with PowerPoint.

But when I led meetings, I felt uncomfortable with everyone's focus on me. I worried about whether I was making sense. A voice in my head would start in on me: *Who the hell do you think you are? You're sitting here like you know exactly what's going on, but you aren't shit because nobody knows who you really are. You're just a loser who survived the last 15 years of your life, who lived with a drug addict, whose husband had HIV. You're an imposter, a fake, a phony. People are looking at you like you've got it together, but you know the truth: you're nobody.*

My inner critic would hammer away at me, causing me to short circuit and lose my train of thought. As a result, I'd sometimes pause in the middle of my presentations and hope that someone would chime in and take over.

I convinced myself that if my colleagues, bosses, and clients knew the truth about me and my life, they'd look at me differently. I also worried that I was mentally ill, just like my parents. My therapist had diagnosed me with post-traumatic stress disorder as a result of Larry's drug use and illness, but therapy wasn't providing me with any relief. I couldn't comprehend the enormity of the sadness I felt, and the PTSD could send me into a panic so easily.

I recall lying in a hammock in my backyard one day and looking up at the sky. I started to have a conversation in my head with the universe. *What will it take to make this hurting stop?*

Yet, even with my self-doubts and emotional difficulties, I was promoted to vice president of sales at my company. Me—the girl who never thought she was smart enough or good enough! My father was immensely proud of me. "My daughter was once on welfare, but now she's a vice president!" My life was one big contradiction.

The boys and I tried to do the best we could to keep going, but every major life event was painful. When the kids graduated from different grades or received awards, their dad wasn't there. Someone in the family would get married, and Larry wasn't there. I'd receive an accolade at work, and my husband wasn't there to hear about it. I hated being solo. I missed my friend and partner.

After a couple of years, my friends said I should think about dating again. *Who's going to love me?* I thought. If I started dating someone, it would be hard enough to be a fortysomething widow, but how could I tell a man that my husband had had HIV? That was a recipe for getting rid of a guy, not attracting one. Who would want to have a relationship with a woman whose husband had died of what was seen as a highly contagious plague?

I'd go out to a bar with girlfriends now and then, and if a man approached me, he'd ask if I was single. When I said yes, I'd get, "So, have you been married?"

"Yeah."

"Divorced?"

"No."

"Separated?"

"No."

"Well, what did he do, die?"

"Yeah."

"Oh, man, I'm sorry." Then the guy wouldn't be able to get away from me fast enough.

So I chose to remain secretive. Keeping my secrets gave me an excuse to keep most everyone at arm's length. For years after Larry's death, my family, Larry's family, and Debbie remained the only people who knew what had really happened.

As my grief continued without letting up, my sons got older. Larry, Jr., entered high school, and I worried, as I'm sure most parents do, about his increased independence. When he was 14—a couple of years after Larry's death—I discovered that he was hanging out with some older kids who could drive and were drinking beer. I saw him take off in a car with them and began to panic. It triggered my PTSD, making me feel that my eldest son might go down the same path his father had and end up dead. So I became very protective of and strict with him.

One day, while in the car together shortly after that incident, I was lecturing Larry, Jr., and wound up blurting out the truth about his dad. "You know, your father was no angel! He had a drug problem."

At first, my son didn't respond. He froze, trying to comprehend what he'd just heard. The cat was out of the bag, so I pulled over, stopped the car, and continued. "Look . . . your dad was a drug addict. He left us when you were a baby and was living on the street for a while. He got HIV from shooting drugs. It killed him! Do you have any idea what that did to his life and what will happen to you if you get involved with alcohol or drugs? He ruined our lives!" I lost control of my emotions and began to sob. "Don't you see that? And his sister and brother were drug addicts too. It runs in the family. It's the Crawford curse. Larry, you can't fool around with drugs or alcohol! Your genetics are against you. And if anything ever happened to you, I would die. Don't you know that?" Then my son joined me in my sobbing.

Losing control like that scared the life out of me. It reminded me of my father's screaming outbursts. Was I so damaged that I would become like my dad when he was younger?

Words can't express how terrible I felt for telling my son in this way. It wasn't at all the way I had envisioned telling him. I know that day redefined him and caused him enormous pain, because his image of his dad was shattered. But it was also the day that brought me to my knees and made me aware that I had to get real help. The therapy I'd received up to that point obviously hadn't been working.

I didn't want Larry, Jr., to tell anyone else, especially his little brother, so in telling him, I inadvertently made him join me in my secret-keeping. I felt terribly guilty about it, and probably always will. Larry, Jr., whom I had vowed to protect, had inherited my caretaking role when his father was alive, and he was now also inheriting my secrets.

CHAPTER 9

ENDINGS AND
NEW BEGINNINGS

So many things could trigger a memory that would bring me to my knees: Hearing songs that my husband and I had shared. Seeing fathers with their sons. Or just the arrival of a Sunday morning, since that's when our whole family would always spend time together.

Then there was the smell of lumber—the familiar scent that I associated with Larry as he rebuilt our home. Not long after his death, I made the mistake of trying to shop at The Home Depot and became stricken with my feelings of loss. We'd spent so much time there together, buying supplies and materials for the house and for his work, that it was like hallowed ground. We had always enjoyed picking out what we'd use to design our home. I hadn't realized that being there would bring up such intense longing for him. It would be years before I could bear to shop there again.

Reluctantly, I spoke to my therapist, Pat, about trying psychiatric pharmaceuticals. She didn't usually advocate using medication for mental health, but she had to concede that I wasn't improving. I was only falling deeper into darkness. She sent me to a psychiatrist, who could provide a prescription.

First, I was given Prozac, but it didn't help at all. Instead, my thoughts became even more chaotic. I was desperate, however, so I kept trying. Next was Lexapro, Wellbutrin, Xanax, and lithium. The lithium worked, but I felt so lethargic that I couldn't function. I took it for a few weeks because it did bring me some relief from the mood swings, but I wouldn't have been able to work if I'd continued taking it.

When the meds failed me, I didn't know what else to do but focus on my work and my boys. I had worked hard to create a safe space where Brian and Larry, Jr., could acknowledge their grief, feel happy, sad, or angry. I wanted them to be patient with and kind to themselves.

The irony was that I couldn't do the same for myself. Even though my career was going very well—I had a solid reputation in my tough and competitive industry and was managing millions of dollars of business—I still felt like I had a big *L* for "Loser" stamped on my forehead.

Years went by as being grief-stricken, thinking of myself as a loser, and going through the motions simply became the norm for me. When I took the boys somewhere, I usually sat on the sidelines deep in thought as they enjoyed themselves on their own. They tried to lift my spirits, and they often managed to do so for short periods of time. It was beautiful how concerned they were about me. But when I was alone, I nearly always descended back into the darkness.

I was exhausted from all the responsibility on my shoulders. At the time, I wasn't aware that continuing to keep Larry's secrets was yet another responsibility that I had imposed upon myself. It had simply become a way of life, and since I no longer had to hide the progression of Larry's illness or answer questions about his death, I didn't question the wisdom of keeping the truth to myself.

I did everything I could to compensate for the fact that my sons had to live with a depressed mother. It was important to me to encourage them to experience life adventurously, so I began a new family tradition of taking them on winter vacations during their school breaks. A few years after Larry's death, I took us all on a rain forest vacation package in Venezuela. The boys enjoyed it, but every trip we took pushed me further into my despair. I saw women with husbands and families with fathers. Strangers assumed I was divorced, and this made me want to scream, "I'm not a single parent by choice! I didn't sign up for this life!" The word "widow" made me cringe.

When we returned from Venezuela, I began to experience gastrointestinal problems, and before I knew it, I'd dropped 30 pounds. For a year, I went to several specialists, including a gastroenterologist, but the test results were always inconclusive. The doctors wanted to attribute all my symptoms to grief or work stress. It was infuriating that they wouldn't listen to me.

Then other symptoms began. I experienced chest pain, insomnia, brain fog, and, worst of all, frequent migraines with an aura that affected my eyesight. Debbie suggested that I see Dr. Marton. I hadn't seen him since Larry's death and had always thought of him as Larry's doctor. He was an infectious disease specialist, so I wondered if he'd even agree to see me. But he did.

When he walked into the examining room, tears began rolling down my face. Every memory of Larry's experiences in doctors' offices came flooding back. On the one hand, it was painful, but I was also happy to see this dedicated physician and caring man who had been so important in our lives.

He immediately took charge and dug deep, running every test imaginable on me. In no time, he discovered that I'd been infected with a variety of amoebas while in South America. It explained practically all my symptoms. He started treating me right away, and I was ecstatic to be on my way back to good physical health.

But then another of the tests came back with a diagnosis we didn't expect. I also had hepatitis C, and my liver function had already diminished.

At his office on the day he told me, Dr. Marton continued to try to explain the medical details, but I couldn't hear him or comprehend what he said. All I could think about was the boys. Was I going to die and leave my boys orphaned by *a different disease* after managing to escape HIV? Not after everything they'd already been through! It just couldn't be! How could my luck be so terrible? Suddenly I had more of an understanding of how Larry had felt when he received his diagnosis.

"How did I get it?" I asked.

"Almost certainly from Larry," Dr. Marton said. "It can stay dormant in the body forever, or it can become active after about 20 years."

Obviously, the antibody that had protected me from HIV hadn't protected me from hep C, and I still don't understand why the previous tests had never detected the disease in my system.

"Dr. Marton, can I die from this?" I asked, dreading the answer.

He looked at me with kindness. "I won't let anything happen to you."

While I knew he meant it, I also knew he might not be able to keep that promise. Once again, I was terrified. I couldn't believe that I was still haunted by the repercussions of addiction years after Larry's death. My anger toward my husband came back in full force, but I felt guilty for feeling it. But my main concern would always be my sons, so I knew I had to do everything I could to get well.

Dr. Marton suggested that we check the progress of the hep C monthly. As he'd done for Larry, he wanted to avoid starting me on the existing treatments for as long as we could and wait for new drugs to be developed. The treatment protocol at that time would have been almost the same as the treatment for HIV, and I already knew what those side effects were like. How would I be able to take care of my boys if I got sick from the medications?

Dr. Marton was able to help my body rid itself of the amoebas from Venezuela, and I worked with a doctor of Chinese medicine as well. I gained the weight back, and my gastrointestinal symptoms subsided. That left the symptoms of hep C, which were mainly chronic fatigue and brain fog. I was able to function, but it was a challenge to remember sales numbers and the many details needed in my job, especially since I worked for one of the most demanding companies in the industry.

I did my best to hide that I was ill and not 100 percent on my game. Just as I had always done, I put one foot in front of the other, hid what was really going on, wore a brave face, and kept going the best I could.

While it was especially difficult to travel so much when I didn't feel healthy, that was simply part of the job. Since there were five years between them, Larry, Jr., entered high school while Brian was still in elementary school. They were the latchkey kids of a single mom, and they no longer needed someone with them 24 hours a day when I was traveling. But I always arranged for someone to look in on them and help them with dinner daily, and I hated being away from them.

About three years after Larry died, I was on a business trip when the boys and I experienced another loss. This time, it was our dog, Max, who had been such a comfort after Larry's death.

Poor Brian was only 10 years old at the time, and he found Max's body in our garden.

My cell phone rang. "Mom, something's wrong. I think Max is dead!"

"What do you mean, Max is dead?"

"Why does everything have to die when you're not home?" my little boy asked.

His words pierced my heart. I felt tremendous guilt that I wasn't there yet again, and I jumped on the first flight back. I remembered how tightly Brian had held me at his father's funeral. I could hear how scared he was when we'd spoken about Max.

Our neighbor was looking in on the boys while I was away, so he helped them bury Max in the backyard. At first, Brian was upset and freaked out about burying the dog, so he called me again. "What do you mean, they're going to dig a hole and put Max in the ground?" he asked me.

His father had been cremated, and we still had the ashes in the house. So Brian had never been to a cemetery. I don't think he'd even thought about what usually happens to bodies after death. Our neighbor lovingly talked Brian through it so he would feel comfortable with the burial.

Ultimately, both of my sons handled Max's death well, but the experience made me feel inadequate as a single parent. I needed someone who could help me raise my boys, not just babysit, as family and friends were willing to do. What they needed were guidance and stability, especially when my work took me out of town.

Around that time, a man named Jerry entered our lives. He was Larry, Jr.'s high school history teacher and football coach. One day, Jerry said to my son, "I see your mom picking you up, but I never see your father. I guess your parents are divorced?"

"No, my dad died."

"Oh, I'm sorry. My father died too, when I was a kid."

The two of them talked about what it's like to grow up without a dad.

When I picked Larry up from school that day, Jerry approached me. "Mrs. Crawford, I had no idea that Larry lost his dad. I really commend you for always being here and staying involved, because I know it's hard to be a single parent. If there's anything I can ever do to help, just let me know."

"Well, how do you think Larry is doing?" I asked Jerry. "I'd really like to know how he is when he's at school and at practice."

"I think he's doing pretty well. He seems happy and gets along with everybody."

After a few more conversations during football season and getting to know each other a bit, Jerry and I went out for a casual drink. Then he asked, "Would you like to do this again?" And we started dating.

He seemed "normal." Unfortunately, I still believed that word had some actual meaning. Now I know better. As Alfred Adler once said, "The only normal people are the ones you don't know very well."

But even if "normal" is a myth, Jerry was the opposite of Larry, which seemed like a good thing at the time. He was stable and as bread-and-butter as they come—something I thought would be good for me. He was a jock, which was the kind of guy I'd always despised in high school. In his younger days, Jerry had been a WWF wrestler, so even physically, he was entirely different from tall and thin Larry. *The edgy, hip, sophisticated guy didn't work, so let's try the jock*, I guess I thought.

Over a period of months, Jerry and I became serious, and he wanted to get married. I hadn't yet told him about Larry's drug use and HIV status, so I knew it was about time that I did. He was taken aback, but since we were all healthy, it didn't frighten him away. Dr. Marton had assured me that the chances of Jerry contracting hep C from me were miniscule, especially if we were careful.

The problem was that I wasn't ready to get married. By this time, Larry had been gone for nearly four years, yet I was still in mourning. I didn't feel that enough time had passed. It seemed like marrying someone else would be disrespectful to Larry's memory. I told Jerry that if I did marry him, I wouldn't give up my last name of Crawford. I used the excuse that the boys would hate it if they had a different name than me.

Despite my reservations, I couldn't deny that there were a lot of good reasons to marry Jerry. First, I was in my 40s and dreaded the idea of dating. Second, I assumed he'd lose interest if I said no, and third, I didn't want to live with him out of wedlock.

"I can't believe you're doing this!" Larry, Jr., said to me, mortified that I would even consider marrying his football coach. "I'll wind up in therapy over this one, for sure."

Brian, on the other hand, fell in love with Jerry and came out of his shell a little bit as a result of their relationship. That was probably the main reason I fell for Jerry. And I expected that Larry, Jr., would come around.

My parents were all for the wedding, but not my friend Debbie. She was adamant that I not marry Jerry and did her best to talk me out of it. "Come on, Kathe, you know you're not in love with him. Jerry's a good guy, but he's not right for you!" I knew she was right, but all I could think about was that I had a chance to give my sons a male role model. I wanted so much to give them a good life.

I thought Jerry might finally offer the emotional support I needed. So we tied the knot in 1999.

At first, I enjoyed the stability of a drama-free life with Jerry. I didn't have to worry about him walking in the door high on drugs. But a month after our wedding, I panicked. I felt like I was losing my identity. I said to Jerry, "I can't do it. I can't be married. We have to get a divorce."

Understandably, Jerry felt very hurt and was adamant that he didn't want to split up. He told me he loved me and that I was just experiencing some jitters that would soon pass.

All I could think was, *Who am I to hurt such a decent guy? Who am I to throw love away?* So I stayed with him. But in time, there was no escaping that the two of us had very little in common. Living with Jerry felt like still living alone. Our marriage showed me how much I'd truly been in love with Larry.

After I'd been seeing my therapist, Pat, for several years, she finally gave up, realizing that she'd tried everything in her arsenal to ease my grief and the negative voices in my head. "I'm sorry, Kathe. Clearly, I can't help you," she said. "I think you have post-traumatic stress disorder and need to find someone else for treatment."

Was I a hopeless case? *Surely I'm not doomed to despairing for the rest of my life!* I thought.

I was willing to dig deep and work hard. I didn't want to be like my mother, who had spent most of her adult life in therapy but was only willing to change up to a point. I was determined to feel whole, whatever it took.

Luckily, that's when a friend recommended a therapist named Jack. He helped me realize that I wasn't at fault in my troubled marriage with Jerry and encouraged me to end it. He was my advocate, acknowledging my career success and telling me I was capable of anything I set my mind to. He often commended me for raising such great children.

At first, it was difficult for me to take in his praise. It certainly wasn't at all how I felt about myself, but Jack was very patient with me. He spent a lot of time digging deeply into my childhood. He couldn't get over my mother's narcissism, and he taught me to understand her more clearly, as well as the behavioral patterns I had developed along the way.

He helped me see how I had denied the trauma and chaos that I experienced as a kid. I always rushed to say, "I've forgiven my parents. They did the best they could." Even from a young age, a part of me understood that everything happens for a reason, so why place blame? But Jack helped me recognize that parts of me were still hurting from what I'd experienced. No matter how deeply I loved my mom and dad, those parts of me needed to acknowledge their pain and anger.

"You won't heal until you accept the truth about how much they hurt you, especially your mother," he said. I began to understand that when my mother rejected me, it hadn't meant that I was unworthy of her love. It had been because she was hurting too. Her behavior toward me really had been about herself, not about me.

The work with Jack helped me begin to resolve some of the issues from my childhood. But I still couldn't quite bring myself to ask Jerry for a divorce . . . not yet.

All the while, my mother had started to become frail and was diagnosed with a chronic lung disease, COPD, from smoking cigarettes throughout her life. She even had to drag an oxygen tank along wherever she went.

"I don't think she's going to last much longer," my father told me.

I knew my mother was determined to die before my dad because she felt she couldn't survive without him. "Joe, you're not going to leave me alone!" she'd say.

The severity of her illness plunged me right back into the depths of my grief over Larry. It also took me back to my childhood, when I'd worried that she would die.

My mother was in and out of the hospital, struggling to breathe and suffering from terrible pain, but the doctors didn't seem to know what to do for her. They kept sending her back home.

One day, my father started to cry. I'd never seen him cry like that before. "I can't take care of her anymore. I don't know what to do. You have to help me. Please!"

"I'm here, Dad. Don't worry, I'll help you. We'll figure this out."

In that moment, I stepped back into my official role as my mother's caregiver and took charge. When I walked into Mom's hospital room that day, she was so relieved and happy to see me. "Please, please, you have to take care of me, Kathe," she pleaded. "You're the only one who knows how to talk to the doctors and get straight answers from them." I had been her advocate with doctors even as a child—an experience that had served me well during Larry's illness.

"Of course, Mom," I assured her.

"You've always been able to see how sick I am. You've always believed me. You've always been there for me." It was amazing to hear this from her after so many years.

Once again, the doctor wanted to send her home despite her suffering. "We can't find anything wrong with her," he said.

After I complained profusely, a nurse called another doctor to examine Mom. While we were waiting for him, however, my mother fell into a coma.

After the new doctor examined her, his news was entirely different from that of the previous doctor. "Your mother probably has no more than 24 hours to live."

Considering how much she'd been suffering, we knew instinctively that this doctor was telling the truth. We caught our breath and faced it as best we could.

Come evening, I experienced surprising closure with her. Everyone who had come to visit my mother went home for the night, except for me and Dad, and we planned to sleep in Mom's room. Around 5 A.M., she came out of her coma and called out to me to sit next to her. We hadn't expected her to ever wake up, but there she was, as coherent as if she'd just awakened from a short nap.

"My Kathe, sweet angel," she said, "I have to tell you before I go that I want you to know how much I love you and appreciate you for taking care of me and for always loving me." Then she held me like I'd wanted her to hold me throughout my whole life. "I'm sorry. Know that I love you so much. You were the mother to me, you know." For the first time, I felt acknowledged for all I'd done for her. It made me feel proud of who I was, and my heart filled with such love for her.

Clearly, she loved me more than she'd been capable of showing when I was a child. It was just that her demons had gotten in the way of her expressing her love during most of her life.

I can't describe the healing I experienced at hearing those words. It was the greatest gift she could have given me, and it certainly helped solidify the work I was doing with Jack.

When everyone arrived at the hospital later that morning, they were shocked to find Mom awake. She had a chance to say good-bye to all of them.

Nearly every person in my life was in that room. It was a prism of my life, and they were all the facets, reflecting back to me the person I'd been and the person I'd become. I looked around at my relatives, my brother and sister, my father, my sons . . . and Jerry. My stomach turned. He didn't belong; he was an outsider. I realized I'd never really let him in, and staying with him wasn't right. I didn't want to be married anymore, even though by this time we'd been married for more than five years.

It was an epiphany that I knew would lead to more than just a divorce. It would change everything.

I'd been trying to build a life based on external factors—relationships with others, a home, and a career—thinking that these externals would bring me happiness. But now, I could see that what I'd built wasn't controllable or sustainable. I had to stop living in the past and stop trying to control the future. I needed to start from where I was and live in the moment.

A short time later, Mom fell into a coma again and passed away. It was my birthday in 2005.

You might think that that would make me sad, but oddly, it felt right. Her death on that day is significant for me. She gave me life on the day I was born and a rebirth to begin my new life on the same day on the calendar.

We all grieved immensely, but at the same time, there was a big sense of relief because a lot of our family drama went with her. My father was even able to reconcile with his brother, who had been persona non grata while my mother was alive.

As was typical of me, I couldn't bring myself to make the break with Jerry right away, even though I'd made the decision to tell him I wanted a divorce. By that time, we were living together mostly as friends, and we didn't really have a marriage anymore.

The year after Mom's death, tests showed that my hepatitis C had advanced to stage 3, and my liver would almost certainly develop cirrhosis if I didn't get treatment right away. So began my experience with the same antiviral drugs that I had watched Larry take.

The breadbox was again filled with prescription bottles. This time, however, I didn't keep the diagnosis from my sons. I explained to them what was happening. The treatments were difficult, and I needed them to be there for me. Larry, Jr., was already 23 by this time, and Brian was 18, so they were mostly taking care of themselves and were happy to help me as I recovered. Jerry was also helpful and supportive.

Part of the treatment involved giving myself injections in my belly every few days. This meant I had to go on business trips with the syringes in my suitcase. For days after each shot, I'd feel horrible and would go into an almost coma-like sleep state. It was difficult to keep working while on the medication, and equally difficult to pretend that everything was okay. I was nothing if not a trooper, however, and through it all, I kept this additional secret about my own illness from my co-workers. I was an expert secret-keeper, and I felt I couldn't risk losing my job.

For nearly a year while I was on the meds, my weekends were spent asleep on the couch. Some of my hair fell out, and my skin itched. I'd feel the itching while asleep, but the injections paralyzed me. I'd fight to move and try to wake up, but I couldn't even move my hands to scratch.

During the last month of the treatment, I developed drug-induced lupus and about 20 lesions that looked like large boils all over my body. It was difficult to walk, and my joints hurt. I did recover, but it took a couple of years to get my strength back, for the lupus to resolve, and for the lesions to go away. It took even longer for my hair to grow back completely, and I went into early menopause. All of this added to my PTSD, but in spite of it, I was determined to improve my life and put all of the turmoil behind me.

Maybe that determination is what finally gave me the courage to tell Jerry I wanted a divorce. "Where do you expect me to go?" he asked me. That's how much he'd come to rely on me to take care of him. He did everything he could to delay the hearings, but the divorce was final after nine years of marriage.

Nine years—that's how long I stayed with someone I didn't really want to marry in the first place.

One of the blessings in my life after Jerry left was my father. We had grown closer after my mother's death. "I know I wasn't around for you during most of your life, but I'm here now," he said. We were together nearly every day, and he gave me the emotional support I needed. I went to his house for dinner, or he came to my house and had dinner with us. We had great in-depth conversations about politics and all sorts of topics. It was then that I realized how much Larry had been like my dad.

Then Dad started having symptoms. We discovered that he had a tumor in his bladder, as well as bone cancer that had gone undiagnosed for years and spread throughout his body.

I'd been fulfilling the dream of being with my father without my mother's interference for the first time in my life. It was like I'd gone back in time and been able to pick up where life had somehow gotten so screwed up for me in childhood. We had four years together after Mom's death, but it felt like such a short time to enjoy our closeness. Still, I was filled with enormous gratitude for whatever time we had to love each other so fully. It was just difficult, after so much loss, to get the news that he was going to die in a matter of weeks.

Dad died the day before my mother's birthday in 2009. I always say she called him home to celebrate with her.

By the time Dad passed away, my nest was empty. Brian was 21 years old and at college. Larry, Jr., was 26 and planning to get married! My mother was gone. My father was gone. Larry was gone. Jerry was gone. Nobody needed me. And even though the work I'd been doing for years with Jack had helped me heal to some degree, underneath it all, I still felt broken and alone.

With everyone gone, there was only one person left to "fix"—me. That's when my focus truly turned to healing myself and finding my voice.

What I didn't yet realize was that I'd never be able to find my voice unless and until I released my secrets. Through all the years after Larry's death, I'd continued to hold them locked in a safe inside myself. My immediate family, Debbie, Jerry, and a few doctors were still the only people who knew. Brian had become an adult, but he still didn't know about his father's drug addiction or HIV.

It wasn't until I began to dig more deeply into my healing process that I discovered how much the secrets were eating away at me inside.

CHAPTER 10

MELTING THE BARNACLES AWAY

When you grow up surrounded by dysfunction and chaos, you develop a constant longing to be loved and nurtured. So it's common to try to capture love by taking care of *others*. In my case, it started with my mother and became my default practice. No surprise, then, that it happened again with both of my husbands. What I had to learn was to love myself and stop looking for someone else to do it.

I was tired of the "if only" game I played with myself. *If only* Larry hadn't been an addict; *if only* Larry hadn't died; *if only* I hadn't married him; *if only* I'd had different parents; *if only* I'd gone to a regular college. *If only* I was better, smarter, and perfect, the people in my life would have loved me and not hurt me.

I still felt like I had to hide in order to be accepted, but one thing I had learned from reading spiritualism books was that the only way my life would change course was if *I* changed course. I finally understood that it didn't have anything to do with the other people in my life, the house I lived in, or my work accomplishments. It was all up to me.

I began to feel frustrated in my work with Jack, however. There was still a great deal of lingering trauma from both my childhood and Larry, and I couldn't seem to stop blaming and shaming myself.

By this time, 12 years had passed since Larry's death. "When am I going to feel better?" I asked. "I get all of this intellectually, and I truly appreciate the growth I've experienced while working with you. But I want so much to move forward. I want to find a way to be happy now. How do I heal my heart? How do I stop my mind? Why am I still hurting so much after all these years?"

Jack didn't have answers for me. Instead, he reached toward his shelf and pulled out a book called *Awakening from Grief* by Ramananda John E. Welshons, with a foreword by Wayne Dyer. John is a teacher, a counselor, and an expert on grief and loss. He was part of the late-1960s spiritual movement and traveled with Ram Dass and other prominent teachers. He studied with Elisabeth Kübler-Ross, and has practiced meditation for decades.

John's book was life changing and read like a road map back to life. I felt as though he had reached into my soul and articulated exactly what I was feeling. Most importantly, I felt that he understood what I needed.

During my next appointment with Jack, I handed the book back to him. "Thank you so much for loaning me this book. This is the kind of therapy I need. Everything he wrote about is what I'm feeling. Please, can we do this kind of work together? Please!"

Jack opened the book and looked at John's biography in the back. "Well, he lives right here in New Jersey. Why don't you get in touch with him?"

When I discovered that John was facilitating an in-person meditation series, I signed up immediately. As I introduced myself to him, my eyes filled with tears. I was overwhelmed by the energy I felt from him. It was the kind of connection I'd been searching for my whole life, and I knew immediately that he held the key to mending my broken heart.

Learning meditation with John was when my journey to an open heart truly began. In private sessions with him, I told him all the things I'd been doing to try to heal. "I'm in therapy, I'm reading and studying, I'm spending time in nature, and I'm running. I'm improving a bit, but nothing's really working to free me from the loss and grief."

"That's because your heart isn't open," John said. That's when he described the barnacles encasing my heart.

"No, no," I said. "When Larry died, my heart exploded into a million pieces! My heart shattered. I'm *so* open!"

"It might have shattered, but it didn't open," he responded.

With patience and kindness, John explained that the barnacles around my heart had been building since childhood like a shield of protective armor. It was a survival mechanism, but those barnacles also closed me off from my own love and from fully receiving the love of others.

It took me a while to accept that my heart was as closed as John said. He just waited patiently for me to come to my own realization about it.

To heal, I needed to dig through all the darkness and hurt I'd neatly tucked away. I was afraid to go inside, but I was more afraid to stay as I was. So with John by my side, I allowed myself to fully feel the pain and let it move through me. I no longer fought the grief. My chest throbbed as the layers over my heart slowly began to crack. I could almost feel those barnacles breaking apart and melting away. Only this time, my heart wasn't shattering.

One of the issues John discussed with me was attachment and how it gets us into trouble. "Everybody's gone!" I protested. "What do I have left to be attached to?"

"You're attached to your pain, your thoughts, and your story," he explained. I began to see that it's easier to stay attached and stuck because we fear the unknown. We're comfortable with the familiar, even if the familiar is awful. But we waste so much energy staying in miserable circumstances simply because it's what we know. How many times in my life had I done that? How much did I deny myself because I didn't believe I deserved more?

For years, my self-worth had depended on approval from others and career success. If I accomplished something, what were the results? Did I do it well or not? If not, it fed my self-doubt. With my self-worth so contingent upon performance, I could fall from my own grace too easily.

Even my best friend, Debbie, had tried to penetrate my self-loathing. "I don't understand why you're so hard on yourself. Why do you hate yourself so much? Why can't you see the good in you? You aren't who you're describing."

My sons also saw me differently from the way I saw myself. They knew what I'd been through and even wrote papers in school about how much they admired me. After all the mistakes I felt I'd made, it was amazing to discover how much the boys loved me.

Yet I still struggled to feel safe enough to come out of hiding and let my true self be seen by anyone but the people closest to me.

John helped me realize that I needed to let go of being a victim. If anybody had told me years before that I was playing the victim, I would have argued, "No! Everything that happened to me was based on my circumstances. I had no control over addiction, mental illness, or death!" But it had been my choice to take responsibility for everyone else's life rather than to take responsibility for my own. I had to face up to the poor choices I'd made over and over out of fear rather than faith. And I had to find compassion within myself for the person I was—a person who didn't yet have the wisdom to make better choices.

It had always been so easy for me to extend compassion toward others. As I learned to give it to myself as well, a few more barnacles broke free, and my self-hatred softened. I started to taste the relief I'd been desperate for. Maybe if I continued my healing process, I'd finally come out of hiding.

As I continued working with John, I attended workshops with a number of spiritual teachers and explored Buddhist and Tibetan traditions. Yoga became another instrumental aspect of my healing. I gave up running five miles a day and learned to be kinder to my body. I enjoyed the flow of my asana (posture/pose) practice and how it connected me with my body.

I attended a workshop at the Kripalu Center for Yoga & Health in Massachusetts that turned out to be an awakening experience for me. I was proud of myself for going alone. I felt so empowered that I'd taken another big step, even though I hadn't known what to expect.

What I discovered was a whole community of people who were searching, just like me. They were involved in all kinds of exciting healing modalities, some of which I hadn't even heard of. I met Reiki masters and other energy healers, Ayurvedic practitioners, and specialized massage therapists. I began adding some of what I learned from them into my own practice as I realized that this kind of community could expose me to the wide variety of therapies available for healing.

I also went on a retreat at the Sivananda Ashram in the Bahamas and met a Vedic priest from South America who did a Vedic birth chart for me, which is a karmic map that shares the wisdom of life in the past, present, and future. Most of my friends and family thought I'd gone off the deep end by exploring spiritual healing, and I wanted to know if I was on the right path.

The reading showed that I was born under a dark moon. Since birth, I'd been in search of the light. The priest said I'd spend my entire life seeking truth. "You need to stop resisting the calling and learn to embrace your gifts."

"But what is my truth? What's my calling?" I asked.

"Your calling is to teach, to heal, and to help others, but you have to heal yourself first. To thine own self be true."

"But I'm so frustrated. I can't seem to heal my heart."

"Stay connected to your heart. It needs to open." I knew he must be right if he was telling me exactly what John had said.

"Deepen your practice of Bhakti yoga," he continued. "Include chanting, mantra, and prayer in your practice, and your heart will open through your love and devotion. It will guide you on the path to self-realization, bringing you closer to God—to oneness."

I did as he suggested, and slowly, I began to find peace on my mat. "Yoga" means "union," and that's how it felt for me. While on the yoga mat, my body, mind, and breath flowed seamlessly in union. I could dance with my soul, with the energy of life, and with the flow of grace. My heart filled with gratitude and bliss.

Yoga quickly became my sacred time and space. I was able to disconnect from my responsibilities and the noise that surrounded me. The negative thoughts didn't rule me. *So this is what peace feels like!* I thought. I felt so connected to myself, grounding my feet to the earth and rising high to touch the heavens. I felt a contentment that I hadn't experienced before.

When I was in yoga class, I didn't care what was happening around me. I didn't care if the other students were standing on their heads or if I was moving through a position correctly. It brought me such joy that I felt nothing could touch me. At the same time, I was deeply touched by the experience.

During Savasana (corpse pose), I often experienced a healing emotional release. Slowly, the light started to penetrate the darkness. In the beginning, I experienced only faint glimpses of light, but those glimpses kept me going until I experienced them for longer and longer periods of time. Eventually, the light started to overcome the darkness.

I was particularly drawn to the mantras of yoga practice. Since childhood, I had used prayer to get me through tough times, and chanting the mantras became my new way to pray. It was a direct line to the divine that connected me to my own divinity, that transcended any of my negative beliefs about myself and went far beyond what I'd experienced in therapy.

I couldn't get enough. I wanted to spend every minute discovering more. I read the *Bhagavad Gita,* studied the *Yoga Sutras of Patanjali,* and learned the eight limbs of yoga. I practiced the yamas and niyamas, which were the ethical foundations of my spiritual practice. I'd finally found the home I'd been seeking since my childhood, only it wasn't behind closed doors. It wasn't even a physical place. It was inside me. And I wanted to learn everything I could and share it so that more people could have the same wonderful experience.

As a result of my meditation practice, yoga, and therapy with John and Jack, my thoughts and behaviors began to change and become more positive. The ache in my heart softened. I could incorporate the teachings into my day-to-day life. I could stop myself if I judged myself or someone else, compared myself to others, or put others' needs ahead of my own.

Through daily practice, I learned to stop thinking about the past and the future and to stop focusing on outcomes. I stopped thinking of the people in my life as problems or obstacles. I began to see them all as gifts— even the ones who had hurt me the most. I recognized that they'd taught me important lessons.

Gradually I let go of the "if only" game. That thinking had kept me locked in the belief that happiness was contingent upon some outside situation rather than what happiness actually is—*an inside job*. I learned that happiness is a moment-to-moment experience, not some static state that we achieve one day and never have to create again. Happiness can only be experienced in the moment of now . . . and the next moment . . . and the next.

In meditation, I began to see and experience love as a state of *being* rather than *doing*. Gradually, when I closed my eyes and sat on my pillow, I was able to let go of thoughts like "I wish Larry was alive" and "I wish I had that job I always wanted" and "Kathe, you're such a loser." Slowly but surely, I learned how to be present in the moment. The negative voices didn't go away, but I learned to separate them from the truth of who I am. I was beginning to feel again, and my heart was opening. I was so grateful to be alive and grateful that I could see the gifts life had given me.

I had always believed my thoughts, even the negative ones, thinking of them as my steering wheel. Then I woke up and noticed how much my thoughts had controlled me and defined who I was, even though many of those thoughts hadn't belonged to me. They'd been the voices of my parents and others who had put me down over the course of my life. And like we all do, I'd adopted those voices as my own.

My true voice—the real me deep inside—had been drowned out by the cacophony of negative voices that constantly chattered as they tried to keep me in check. When a punishing thought passed through my mind, I no longer allowed it to take over me. I connected to an objective part of myself, a higher state of consciousness that allowed me to see the thought for what it was—a fear, a falsehood that I had once believed. Then I could let it float away on the breath and begin my next inhale, allowing each moment to unfold.

A major shift had occurred inside me. I could forgive myself for being human. That experience grew into stronger self-love and the understanding that we are all pure love in our essence.

When I connected to my breath in meditation, I discovered that the breath is who we are! I kept going deeper inside, and that's where I found the real Kathe in the arms of divine love—the me from before I had a name or any labels attached to me. The me who had been hidden almost my entire life behind a wall of secrets.

The pure love of my essence flowed through me, finally healing my heart and giving me the peace that had eluded me for so many years.

Eventually, I discovered a devoted bhakti community and my beautiful teacher, Sheryl Edsall, at Naturally Yoga in Glen Rock, New Jersey. As I listened to Sheryl's sweet teachings and chants, I could feel my heart opening further. But Sheryl and my classmates still didn't know my story. They were exceptionally loving people, but I was still hiding, fearful that I'd be rejected if they knew the truth.

After taking only two of Sheryl's classes, I decided to take a nine-month teacher training course with her. I wasn't interested in actually teaching yoga; I simply wanted to deepen my knowledge of the spiritual teachings, also known as Jnana yoga.

The training was a huge commitment for me, and I was nervous since I'd avoided commitments after I left my marriage. I didn't know how I would juggle the courses with my demanding job and its travel obligations. And I was dating someone I cared about after years of being alone.

As the training began, Sheryl told us that whatever wasn't meant to be in our lives would fall away during the nine months. I suppose she was right, because five months into the training, the man I was seeing broke up with me abruptly. He just said, "I'm not feeling it anymore," and left. It was yet another hurt and loss in a long list of hurts.

But today, I realize that the universe had my back. He was no more right for me than Jerry had been. It was a solid lesson for me about attachment and love, but at the time, it felt like a big setback. I was an emotional wreck as a result, and it brought all of my abandonment issues right back up to the surface.

This time, however, I had the ability to observe and process my feelings and reactions. I could tell when I was responding from a place of self-doubt and fear. I couldn't always control my fears, but I could at least recognize them. That, in and of itself, was growth.

It was difficult to continue with the training while going through this emotional turmoil, but the training was still a godsend for me. I could process the difficult feelings using the tools I was learning while also receiving my community's support.

Even though I wasn't interested in becoming a yoga teacher, Sheryl and her husband, Neil, encouraged me to think about teaching. "You have a gift and an energy in you," Sheryl said. But I couldn't see what they were talking about, especially since my self-doubt had kicked in again after the breakup.

When graduation day came, our families arrived to celebrate with us. Sheryl shared the stories of three goddesses: Lakshmi, Saraswati, and Durga. Lakshmi brings in abundance, Saraswati represents eloquence with words and creativity, and Durga is the destroyer and protector. Sheryl asked our families and friends to decide which of these goddesses symbolized each one of us. When she called on my sons, they unanimously said that I would be Saraswati. Even before she knew this, Sheryl had already chosen my Sanskrit name, Vani, which means "speaking your truth."

"I'm honored that you see me as eloquent," I said to Sheryl, "but I'm struggling to see it. If only I could find my voice!"

"When you learn to see what others see in you, you'll find your voice," she said.

I sighed. I thought I'd already begun to see what others saw in me, but obviously, I had more work to do.

Some time after the training, my friend Danielle and I visited Yogaville, an ashram and the home of Sheryl's guru, Swami Satchidananda (or Guru Dev, as he's often referred to), in Buckingham, Virginia. He was noted for opening the Woodstock music festival in 1969 and founding Integral Yoga, and he was instrumental in bringing yoga to the West.

We had been told that this ashram, situated within the Blue Ridge Mountains, was a magical place. We were bursting with excitement during our eight-hour ride there. It was like a pilgrimage to the Holy Land.

At first, though, we were disappointed. We didn't feel the magic we'd expected. Then, that night, I had the most vivid dreams filled with beauty and serenity unlike anything I'd ever experienced. I saw myself as a kid walking up and down the street where I'd grown up. I witnessed the conversations I'd had with God as a child, asking Him to watch over me when I felt alone and afraid.

Throughout this movie of my life, I wasn't scared. I felt safe and secure. I felt like everything that had happened to me in my life had brought me to that moment. Something was guiding me through the dream, and I believed it was Swami Satchidananda. After all, I was at his home—his sacred land.

In the morning, Danielle told me she had had amazing dreams too. We compared our experiences, and they were remarkably similar.

That morning, being at the ashram was a completely different experience for me—like heaven on earth. It felt like home. The St. James River runs through the hundreds of acres of the ashram's sacred land, and Danielle and I decided to go kayaking. As I paddled down the river, I thought about my dad and how much we'd enjoyed nature together. As I watched the birds fly overhead, I could feel him with me. I felt joy, peace, and a connection to the divine.

When we returned home, I told Sheryl that she needed to take the yogis from the studio to the ashram. "Everything you've been teaching me makes more sense to me now," I said.

"If you coordinate it and make it happen, I'll go there and teach," Sheryl said. So I did just that, and soon we were holding regular retreats at the ashram.

During the first retreat, I did my Karma yoga work. I served the attendees by washing dishes, making chai, and placing beautiful little lotus flowers on the doors of their rooms. I could tangibly feel the difference between taking care of others from a full heart as opposed to a place of deprivation. It was full-circle love and pure bliss.

During our third retreat at the ashram, another teacher from the studio named Veronica came up to me while I was working in the kitchen.

"Kathe, I don't know if you know much about me. I don't tell many people this, but I'm an intuitive. Sometimes angels speak through me. As I watch you, I see three angels next to you, and they're sending me messages."

"Yes, I know."

"You do?"

"Yes, they're my mother, my father, and my husband, Larry."

"Yes, that's exactly who they are. They have a message for you."

I was excited because over the years, I had gone to a number of psychics who speak to the other side, hoping that Larry would come through. He had only come through briefly a couple of times to say that he was watching over me and the boys. Maybe he would have more to say this time!

"They want you to know that they're with you, but they don't *need* to be with you," Veronica continued. "It isn't that they don't *want* to be with you. But they're only here because you want them here."

"What are you talking about? Why wouldn't they want to be with me? It's the least they can do. I did take care of them! Are you saying that even in death, they don't want to be with me?"

"You're not hearing me. They want you to know that they'll stay as long as you need them, *but you don't need them*! You're okay without them."

"No, no, no! I'm *not* okay without them! Why the hell wouldn't they want to be with me? They left me here!"

Veronica stayed calm and held the space for me as the emotions and the darkness rushed through me.

"You're not hearing me. They'll stay with you, but you need to realize that you don't need them. You're doing the work. You don't need to hold on to them any longer."

She was right; I couldn't hear her. All I could hear was that they were abandoning me *again*! It would take me some time to process Veronica's message from my loved ones. It was yet another lesson about attachment.

At the end of the retreat, Sheryl asked everyone to say a word or two about me in gratitude for coordinating their visit to the ashram. Even with all the work I'd been doing, it was hard for me to take in.

Then Neil spoke. He said, "When I met Kathe, I met someone so filled with love that she's literally *pure love*." His words changed me forever. I trusted Neil. I loved him and felt humbled by what he said. This time, I could truly let the love in.

I had another transformative experience when a new career opportunity came out of the blue. Cartier called me because they knew my work and wanted to interview me for a position. This was the most prestigious watch company in the world!

I had come a long way from my humble beginnings, but this time, I wasn't nervous. I wasn't attached to the outcome. I knew that I was successful whether or not I got hired. Instead, I just felt gratitude. It was the first time in my life that I really owned who I was. All of my inner work on myself was following me into the business world, with no *L* on my forehead anymore.

And I got the job.

After one of our retreats at the ashram, I rode home with Sheryl and Neil. Sheryl pointed out that I hadn't shared many details of my personal life with them. She started asking about Larry.

I was faced with a pivotal moment, and I knew I needed to be honest with Sheryl and Neil. It wasn't fair to them or to me to hide anymore. Was I willing to be vulnerable and give up my false sense of self?

I took a deep breath and told them all of it from beginning to end—Larry's drug years, his struggle with HIV, and his death. It took about three hours of the drive to get through it, and afterward, we were all completely drained emotionally and physically.

They were blown away that I had kept my story hidden from most people for so long—it had been almost 20 years since Larry's death. But in the end, they offered me pure love, no judgments. And they didn't treat me any differently than they had when we had begun our drive.

Then Neil shared some of his personal story, which included a difficult childhood. I realized that I wasn't alone and that we all have stories buried inside of us.

"In the end, your attachment to the story is like a chain that binds you to Larry and your parents," Sheryl said. "You're holding on to something that no longer exists. You're holding it so tight, and it's so heavy that it's dragging you down. Why are you still holding it?"

What she said was so similar to what John had told me, and it harked back to Veronica's message about attachment too. "I don't know, Sheryl. If they're gone, what else do I have? It's all I have. It's all I've ever known. It's who I am."

"It's *so* not who you are! Sweet angel, they were in your life, but they aren't who you are. And *what* happened to you is *not* who you are, Kathe. Until you release that bind, you won't find your voice. You won't ever fully heal your heart. You won't find your happiness or your peace."

Sheryl asked me to close my eyes and envision the binds attaching me to Larry and my parents. "Imagine how tightly you're holding on to them and those ropes. So tight! You need to release those ropes, those binds. You need to let them go!"

I leaned forward from the back seat. "But how do I do that?"

"You need to meditate on it every day until you can release them. I'll give you a mantra to say. Trust me," she said. And I did. I trusted her more than I did anyone.

"Now I understand why you doubt yourself so much," Sheryl said. "Please know that you're a beautiful person with so much to give. You need to teach. Your voice needs to be heard. You're filled with wisdom and experience that can help a lot of people, but you're holding yourself back. You're living in two worlds, and you don't know where you belong. It's time to let go of the old and allow yourself to be fully born."

It was time to truly, finally let go of my secrets.

CHAPTER 11

LIFE WITHOUT SECRETS

In 2013, Brian turned 25 and was a college graduate. Unlike a lot of his friends who were getting married, he didn't have a steady girlfriend. So he asked if he could move back in with me for a while. I enjoyed having him in the house, which had felt empty since he'd moved out.

When he started dating a new girl, I noticed that the two of them were drinking and partying a lot. They would stay out until four, five, or six in the morning on the weekends and sleep all day. Since Brian was into the club scene, I knew drugs like Ecstasy were readily available to him. He was normally very conscientious and had done well in his work as a business analyst, and I knew the signs all too well and could spot a stoner a mile away.

"Are you smoking pot, Brian?" I asked.

At first, he didn't want to admit it, but I pressed him until he told me that he and his girlfriend had been trying club drugs.

"It's no big deal, Mom. Everybody's doing it."

Beside myself with fear, I called Larry, Jr. "What should I do, Larry? Should I tell Brian everything? I'm afraid he's on a bad road, and he has no idea of his history."

"Trust yourself, Mom," he said. "I know it's hard, but you have to tell him."

It was a difficult decision, but I felt my son's well-being was at stake. At that point, everyone who mattered had been told the secret except for Brian. He was the last person left who could be hurt by our story. And I knew how much it was going to hurt him to hear the truth. It brought back memories of the day I'd had to tell him that his father had died. Would it shatter him again to find this out about his dad? It worried me tremendously, and I felt guilty for having kept it from him for so long. Once again, a secret was causing a lot of pain in my family. So I thought that maybe it was time to rip off the Band-Aid.

"We need to talk," I said to Brian. "I'm going to tell you something that's going to redefine your life. I haven't told you this because I never wanted to tarnish your wonderful memories of your father. But now I need to tell you because I can't watch you do this to yourself."

"Wow, Mom, what's wrong?"

"Brian, your dad had a drug problem."

"I figured," he said, but I could tell he didn't understand the seriousness of it.

"No, really! He was a drug addict. He shot heroin for many years."

I told him a bit about his father's drug years, but I think Brian still felt I was merely lecturing him. I wasn't breaking through. His will was strong, and he wasn't going to let me see him sweat.

"Brian, your dad got HIV from a dirty needle. He had HIV and that's what ultimately killed him."

He was silent at first. Then he cried just as hard and as quietly as he had at age seven after his father's death. It broke my heart to watch my son sob like that, but I felt such relief that he finally knew the secret. I'd always feared that if something happened to me, he'd hear it from someone else and feel betrayed. But as long as I kept it from him, I could continue to hide from it. Finally telling him was healing for all of us.

"Wow . . . everything about me and my life makes sense now," Brian said.

"I'm so sorry, Brian. I'm so sorry." I hugged him. "Your dad loved you so much, and I know he's here with us now, wanting to make sure you don't go down the same road. Telling you this is the hardest thing I've ever had to do. But no matter how painful it is, you need to know. You have a right to know.

"If you're addicted, you have to tell me and stop it now! If you have a problem, I'll help you get treatment and support you in recovery, but I won't ever enable another addict. I can't give up who I am. I can't live in darkness again, not even for my son."

It was so difficult to say, and it was only because of all the work I'd done within myself that I could say it. I had to stay in my truth.

Brian gazed into my eyes. I could tell that after learning about what I'd been through and how I'd fought to protect him and his brother, he was seeing me for the first time as more than just his mom.

My secrets had started out as a way of protecting my husband from the stigmas of addiction and HIV. Then I protected my sons from the people who might shut us out if they knew. But I was protecting myself just as much from the ridicule and judgments I was sure would come my way if people saw the real truth, the real me.

It has been a long time coming, but I now realize that I turned my secrets into scarier monsters than they actually were. Yes, there was a terrible stigma attached to drug addiction and to HIV/AIDS for a long time—and there still is, to some degree. Nevertheless, even in the beginning, there were people in our lives who would have understood. They had proved that when I finally had the courage to tell them. Maybe I could have convinced Larry to let us trust someone. But even if he had agreed, would I have trusted someone else enough to do it? Probably not. For so many years, I'd been filled with too much self-doubt and shame.

The day I finally told Brian, I believe the lineage of drug addiction was truly broken in our family. And so was the cycle of dysfunctional secret-keeping.

Since that time, I've learned that even when you believe you're keeping a secret, it isn't necessarily as secret as you think. Years later, my sons admitted to me that once they were told about their dad's addiction, they didn't need me to tell them what he'd done on the last evening of his life.

They'd both figured out that their father had gotten high the night before he died and that he'd probably done it to end his life. Knowing that he hadn't taken drugs just for the sake of getting high gave them comfort. They've told me that they feel compassion for how much pain he was enduring, and as awful as it was for them, they understand why he wanted it to end.

For a long time, I shut down my memories of Larry because I felt paralyzed by them. My story and Larry's story kept me locked in the past. Now, my memories free me. They bring me comfort rather than grief. The longing and emptiness I used to feel have become peace and gratitude. I feel blessed for having had all the experiences of my life.

The day that I stood up at the Omega Institute and gave my talk, I discovered that my experiences contained even more blessings than I had realized. Releasing my story was healing not only for me, but also for others. There were people who understood and related to my experience—people who had also hidden themselves away in secrecy and shame, wanting desperately to have the courage to live in truth.

That reality hit home further when I was on a plane and started a conversation with the woman sitting next to me. When I told her about my book, I mentioned that I had kept a secret about my husband's death for years. "My husband died too," she said.

"What did he die of?"

"I can't tell you. It's a secret I'm not ready to share."

You can't make this stuff up, right?

"I certainly understand that, as you can imagine," I said. "But I'll tell you my secret because it's going to be written in a book soon anyway." I needed to practice saying it out loud because the words still tended to get stuck in my throat. I took a deep breath. "He was a drug addict who contracted HIV from dirty needles."

"Wow. Thanks for that." She paused and looked at me. I could tell she was trying to decide whether or not to tell me her own secret.

"I still don't think I can tell you my story, but if you'll give me your e-mail address, I'd like to write you and tell you about it. If I tell you now, you might feel awkward the rest of the flight."

"Of course. I'll give you my e-mail address and would be happy to hear about it if you want to write to me."

And she did.

However and whenever we choose to tell our secrets, one of the biggest lessons I've learned is that life's too short to live it unauthentically. We only do that because we fear judgment. When we truly love ourselves, we don't worry so much about being judged by others. We can have our own approval, and that's what matters most.

With my story finally out in the open, I feel a huge sense of freedom. It's a rebirth. I can unapologetically be proud of who I am. This is me. And through living my truth, I've been able to help others. In my work as an integrative life coach, I teach people that whatever their story is—however shameful they believe it to be—they don't have to hide behind it. Living in reality is so much better than living in denial. The real you is so much more beautiful than any pretense you can make up.

Like most of us, for a long time, I held on to the identity that had been given to me. This is how we hold on to the negative stories that cause us to play out the same scenarios over and over in life. But I wasn't a difficult child or a phony. I wasn't a misfit. I was and am beautiful, kind, competent, and compassionate. I have come to see myself the way those who love me see me, and my voice has been freed.

I was that little girl who wanted to knock on my neighbors' doors and ask to be loved. But what I really needed was to knock on my own door, open it, and take myself into my own heart.

I recently found a photo of myself at about age 10, and when I look at that little girl, I can vividly remember her pain and her fear that she wasn't lovable. I look at that picture every day, show her some love, and welcome her back home in my heart. Today, I know that I don't just give love to myself or someone else. I *am* love.

See—I told you this was a love story.

ACKNOWLEDGMENTS

We do not find our identity in isolation; we find it from being heard.

Through our voice, we find where we belong in this crazy and wild world.

To everyone I have met along the way, thank you for your friendship, your hand, your heart, your love, your stories.

All of you gave me the strength and courage to tell this story.

Big Love and thanks to my family and friends who continue to support me on my "crazy" spiritual journey. Thank you to my sister Kris, who is never far from my side, and Debbie, who often believes I am absolutely insane. My brother, Joe, I love you.

Sheryl and Neil, for the gift of love and the beautiful sangha at Naturally Yoga.

John Welshons, your love and wisdom melted the barnacles from my heart; thank you for opening my heart.

Jack Schwartz, we spent a lifetime together; thank you for always cheering me on.

Melanie Votaw, your eloquent and beautiful words shine like diamonds in the sky. With kindness and compassion, you held space, and in that space, your brilliance and professional wisdom brought this story to another level.

Nancy Levin, who taught me the art of a graceful exit, you slow me down just enough to hear your words, "Honor the space between 'no longer' and 'not yet.'"

I trusted, jumped, and landed on my feet. Thank you for inspiring me every day.

Patty Gift, I am forever grateful. Nothing happens by chance and I know the universe conspired to bring us together. You pointed me toward the door, encouraged me, and gave me the support I needed to open it. Thank you!!!

Lisa Cheng, your generous feedback and gentle reminder "to dive deeper" allowed my voice, my presence, and the power of the journey to come forward.

Reid Tracy and the amazing team at Hay House, thank you for your support and guidance.

And all the teachers who illuminated the path on my spiritual journey.

Swami Satchidananda, Neem Karoli Baba, Ram Dass, Krishna Das, Louise Hay, Dr. Wayne Dyer, Sharon Salzberg, and The Shambhala Center.

Sarah Tomlinson and Seema Agrawal, thank you for bringing me home to the sacred land of India.

Dr. Marton, no matter how many years pass, I will always call you, Dr. Marton.

You are a brilliant and remarkable man and the most compassionate human being I have ever met. And by the way, you give the best hugs; thank you for being my superhero.

Larry and Brian, you are my pride and joy. Thank you for your love and trust.

I am honored to be your mother.

And to my beloved, Larry, forever in my heart, I will always love you. xoxo

ABOUT THE
AUTHOR

 **Kathe Crawford** is an author, integrative coach, and spiritual teacher. As an inspiring teacher and workshop facilitator, Kathe shares her own story and empowers and guides others to discover and align their own truth. You can visit her online at kathecrawford.com.

Hay House Titles of Related Interest

YOU CAN HEAL YOUR LIFE, the movie,
starring Louise Hay & Friends
(available as a 1-DVD program, an expanded 2-DVD set,
and an online streaming video)
Learn more at www.hayhouse.com/louise-movie

THE SHIFT, the movie,
starring Dr. Wayne W. Dyer
(available as a 1-DVD program, an expanded 2-DVD set,
and an online streaming video)
Learn more at www.hayhouse.com/the-shift-movie

***

BE FEEL THINK DO: A Memoir,
by Anne Bérubé, Ph.D.

A DAILY DOSE OF WOMEN'S WISDOM,
by Christiane Northrup, M.D.

*CONSCIOUS COMMUNICATIONS: Your Step-by-Step Guide to
Harnessing the Power of Your Words to Change Your Mind, Your
Choices, and Your Life,* by Mary Shores

All of the above are available at your local bookstore,
or may be ordered by contacting Hay House (see next page).

***